WORKERS' COMPENSATION IN TWO HOURS

The Business Owner's Guide to an Exceptional Workers' Compensation Program

Nancy Germond, MA, SPHR, SHRM-CP, ARM, AIC, ITP

Wells Media Group, Incorporated

Copyright © 2021 Wells Media Group, Incorporated

All rights reserved

No part of this book may be reproduced, or stored in a retrieval system, or transmitted in any form or by any means, electronic, mechanical, photocopying, recording, or otherwise, without express written permission of the publisher.

ISBN-13: 978-1-7368670-2-0

Printed in the United States of America

CONTENTS

Title Page
Copyright
Introduction — 1
Chapter One - Workers' Compensation – What Are the Benefits? — 6
Chapter Two - Understanding Your Workers' Compensation Policy — 19
Chapter Three - Whether Agent or Broker, Look for the Best — 27
Chapter Four - Reduce Losses with a Strong Safety Culture — 33
Chapter Five - Better Hiring Practices Reduce Injuries and Increase Your Profits — 39
Chapter Six - Safety Training a Key Component in a Safer Workplace — 44
Chapter Seven - Investigating Accidents and Near-Misses Can Help Prevent Recurrences — 48
Chapter Eight - Loss Prevention Committees Help Reduce Accidents and Boost Profits — 55
Chapter Nine - Prompt Injury Reporting Essential in Managing Claim Costs — 63
Chapter Ten - To Reduce Costs, Develop Relationships with Your Adjusters — 69
Chapter Eleven - Nurse Case Management Can Reduce Costs — 78

and Improve Medical Outcomes

Chapter Twelve - Stay-at-Work/Return-to-Work Programs May Provide Your Biggest Savings — 83

Chapter Thirteen - Understanding your Experience Modification Factor — 88

Chapter Fourteen - Surviving the Workers' Compensation Premium Audit — 93

Chapter Fifteen - Emerging Risks and Opportunities in Workers' Compensation — 99

Conclusion — 104

Glossary of Workers' Compensation Terms — 106

About The Author — 113

INTRODUCTION

Why Read This Book?

As a small- to medium-sized business owner, correctly managing your workers' compensation coverage may mean the difference between solvency and filing for bankruptcy. Insurance companies and brokers refer to medium-sized businesses as "middle market." The consulting firm Deloitte defines the middle market as "those making business insurance purchasing decisions at companies with between 26 and 1,000 employees...." Whether you're a small business owner or a middle-market insurance consumer, managing your risk and your insurance purchases gets difficult.

You probably don't have a chief financial officer or a risk manager skilled at understanding insurance coverage and negotiating premiums. It may be difficult for you to find an experienced insurance agent who will help you understand your insurance coverage and manage your risks. Especially if you are a new business start-up, finding an agent can be a frustrating and time-consuming effort.

Workers' compensation insurance is one of the most important yet most misunderstood insurance coverages. Large organizations can hire a risk manager, or their chief financial officer has the expertise to manage their workers' compensation coverage. You, as a small or middle-market business owner, must mainly fend for yourself.

You may be extraordinarily lucky and find an agent or broker who thoroughly understands the workers' compensation underwriting, rating, and claims process. Chances are greater that you will not. Or you may decide to go it alone online with the scores of insurers now offering small business insurance electronically. The online approach to insurance purchases can spell trouble for a growing business.

Some advice in this book will help you choose an agent who understands the workers' compensation policy and process. This will help you tremendously in managing your total cost of risk (TCOR). TCOR is the total expense of managing your risk, including insurance premiums, deductibles, uninsured losses, the indirect loss costs such as administrative time spent managing claims, risk prevention efforts, and more.

This book can make you a smarter insurance consumer, better able to understand the terms and conditions of your workers' compensation policy. It can help you set up a safety program and survive the premium audit you'll undergo each year.

Why You Should Take A Few Hours And Read This Book

You may have heard one or more of the many stories about inadequate insurance advice and simple mistakes in coverage that morph into big problems for business owners. The following brief case study shows just how devastating a mistake in your workers' compensation insurance program can be for your business.

The Business

Robert Smith owned Short-Term Staffing and Short-Term Leasing businesses and other related entities that provided both temporary and leased workers to various industries throughout the Southeastern United States. We changed Mr. Smith's name to protect his identity.

The Situation

In June 20xx, Smith's workers' compensation insurance company insuring both Short-Term Staffing and Short-Term Leasing refused to renew Smith's coverage. His current agent had no other insurance markets willing to write such a large account. This forced Smith to find a new broker. To secure coverage for his companies, Smith met with a broker from a national insurance brokerage. What ultimately resulted was litigation that lasted for years and left Smith in bankruptcy court.

What Happened

The new broker wrote Smith's workers' compensation policy application listing Short-Term Staffing but failed to include Short-Term Leasing on that application. The broker then submitted this incomplete application to the new insurer, which bound coverage for only Short-Term Staffing. Smith mistakenly assumed the workers' compensation policy covered all employees of Short-Term Staffing and Short-Term Leasing.

After the companies' managers filed many both large and small workers' compensation claims, Smith's insurer's personnel found about 60 injury claims filed for employees who were not Short-Term Staffing employees. Instead, they were employees of Short-Term Leasing. The insurer denied coverage for those 60-plus claims.

The Outcome

The insurer opened a fraud investigation into actions taken by Short-Term Leasing managers. Making matters much worse, the US Department of Justice began its own investigation into Smith's alleged premium fraud in August of 20xx. The Federal Bureau of Investigation executed warrants and seized $2.8 million in cash. This forced Short-Term Staffing and Short-Term Leasing into bankruptcy.

Scores of injured employees had no workers' compensation coverage, and litigation began. I worked as an expert witness in this case, estimating the claim value of some of the injured employees. One suffered a mid-foot amputation; another became a quadriplegic after he dove off a dock into shallow water on a $10 bet with his supervisor.

As often happens in litigation, this case had no winners, except perhaps the legal teams. What should have been a relatively uncomplicated insurance transaction bankrupted a business and drew the insurer and the insurance broker into protracted litigation in a U.S. bankruptcy court. It also ended with Smith facing fraud allegations.

What About Your Business?

As you can see, a problem with your workers' compensation coverage can devastate your business. The chaos the owners and managers of these businesses found themselves in provides a warning. Any organization, large or small, should be able to rely on its insurance agent or broker to correctly understand and cover the risks the business faces. But all senior executives should know enough about risk management to ensure they ask the right questions. The health and welfare of the business's most valuable assets – their employees – not to mention the business's financial future, is at stake.

Why Workers' Compensation Coverage?

Workers' compensation coverage is one of the most important coverages you will purchase on behalf of your business. The benefits of a well-run workers' compensation program go far beyond reducing your premiums and increasing your profitability. Here are just a few of the many benefits of a well-run workers' compensation program.

- Your safe workplace creates a stronger bond with your employees. Employees appreciate that you value them and strive to ensure they go home to their families safely each day.

- You help make sure your insurance carrier – your insurer – provides excellent medical care and excels in managing any injuries that do occur. This deepens your relationship with your workers. When you treat injured employees with respect and ensure they receive proper medical care, they can become your best brand ambassadors.

- You experience a reduced chance of problematic Occupational Safety and Health Administration (OSHA) citations or whistleblower complaints from disgruntled employees.

- Your anxiety decreases because you know you hired the best insurance and risk management professionals to guard your business and protect your most valuable assets – your employees.

- Your company develops a solid reputation as an employer of choice as you reduce workplace injuries and improve employee morale.

- You increase the value of your business as you retain top intellectual talent and your reputation as an employer of choice spreads.

In the time it takes you to read this book, you will understand the essential steps to building a solid workers' compensation program. A good program reduces your injury rate and both the direct and indirect costs of workers' compensation losses.

Why not take a few hours to learn more about how to buy your workers' compensation coverage, how to systematize your workers' compensation program, and steps you can take to reduce loss costs before problems arise?

There may be words or terms that are unfamiliar to you. I've tried to explain these terms as we go, but please refer to the glossary if you have questions about a word or term you don't understand.

First, let's examine the benefits payable under your workers' compensation policy.

CHAPTER ONE - WORKERS' COMPENSATION – WHAT ARE THE BENEFITS?

Workers' compensation insurance is the safety net that protects employees when they're hurt after a workplace injury. It also protects the business owner in what experts often call "The Grand Bargain." In that bargain, the injured worker waives his or her right to sue the employer in exchange for medical care, lost wages, rehabilitation, and other statutory benefits.

Statutory benefits refer to the state statutes written by each state that define the payments owed to your injured worker. In this book, we will discuss only state workers' compensation systems, not federal systems such as the Longshore and Harbor Workers' Compensation Act.

According to Chris Archer of Archer & Lassa Law Firm in St. Louis, Missouri, "The cardinal requirement of the workers' compensation law ... is that an employer is liable for the payment of benefits only if an injury or death results from an accident or from an exposure to an occupational disease that arises out of and in the course of an employee's employment." Arising out of employment (AOE) and claims occurring in the course of employment (COE) is the legal standard used to determine if a claim is compensable – payable.

Archer's statement is accurate legally, but it will not cover all the possibilities you and your management team will encounter.

For example, your adjuster denies a claim, but an administrative law judge later finds that claim compensable. Or your adjuster accepts a questionable claim and begins paying benefits to manage the medical portion of the injury to better manage medical and wage loss expenses. This can occur even if you strongly protest the acceptance. This latter example happens frequently. Workers' compensation is a grand bargain when all goes according to plan.

The Workers' Compensation Process

When a claim is work-related, here is a breakdown of the steps in a normal workers' compensation process.

- Step One – The employee has a witnessed or otherwise routine workplace injury or reports an industrial illness, such as lung disease.

- Step Two – Your adjuster investigates the claim, accepts the claim, and begins to manage and pay for the medical treatment, paying lost wages when needed.

- Step Three – When the injury has some extent of lifetime disability or your employee becomes disabled, your employee and your insurer agree in front of an administrative law judge to the degree of disability and the appropriate compensation for that disability.

- Step Four – Your employee and the court accept the final settlement offer.

- Step Five – Your adjuster pursues any subrogation by at-fault parties to recoup payments made on your behalf. Subrogation is a right in your policy that allows the insurer to recover loss payments from the party that caused the loss. For example, the adjuster pursues the insurer of the driver who injures your employee when your employee is blameless.

- Step Six – The adjuster closes the claim. In cases of permanent disability, the adjuster continues to pay "supportive care," court-approved medical care needed for the employee to maintain his or her level of function.

In general, the safety net of workers' compensation operates smoothly, administered slightly differently from state to state. States recognize most types of injury, with back sprains and strains one of the most common work injuries. They also recognize certain occupational diseases, such as asbestosis or certain occupation-related cancers. COVID-19 has added to the complexity of these decisions to accept or deny a workers' compensation claim, known as "compensability determinations."

A compensable claim is one that the insurer or the administrative law judge accepts as work-related and thus payable.

Let's discover the key benefits available under workers' compensation coverage.

The Key Benefits Of Workers' Compensation Coverage

When an employee sustains an on-the-job injury or contracts a work-related illness, your workers' compensation policy responds. Workers' compensation can help provide benefits designed to return your worker to his or her pre-event medical condition. These benefits include the following.

- Medical treatment.
- Wage reimbursement for lost time from the workplace, in most states after a "waiting period." This period can range from three to seven days. The insurer pays no lost wages during that period.
- Future medical and other care and rehabilitation when

needed. If state-mandated or offered voluntarily by the insurer, vocational retraining may occur.

- Death benefits, including funeral expenses and payment to eligible dependents.
- Payment for future disfigurement and disability.

While these benefits are comprehensive, each state administers them according to its state laws. Therefore, what's paid on a claim for a death benefit in California may differ greatly from what the State of Arkansas would require paid.

How Adjusters Calculate Wage Loss

After an injury, your adjuster will request the pre-injury earnings for your injured worker. They use these earnings to calculate either an average weekly wage (AWW) or an average monthly wage (AMW). The calculation varies by state. The insurer typically pays two-thirds of the employee's AWW or AMW, subject to a cap for higher-wage earners. Correctly calculating this wage is important. AWW or AMW is the basis for calculating any future benefits for employees who suffer a permanent partial or permanent total disability.

I introduced an effective rule when I managed a claims team. Each adjuster had to have one other adjuster recalculate and sign off on the adjuster's AWW or AMW calculation. Catching mistakes early means more accurate reserving and no reserve surprises later in the claim's life.

This is a brief overview of the wage loss calculation. It varies greatly by jurisdiction.

A Brief Explanation Of Disability Payments In Workers' Compensation Claims

Depending on the employee's injury, s/he may need income replaced after a loss. Here are the types of temporary disability.

Temporary total disability (TTD) – Paid when the employee is unable to return to work in any meaningful fashion. The AWW or AMW determines the amount paid for the duration of the TTD.

Temporary partial disability (TPD) – The employee continues to treat for his or her injury. However, the employee can return to work with reduced wages. For example, the employee may work half days, or the employer may assign the employee to a lesser-paid position.

Adjusters use two other terms after the employee reaches maximum medical improvement (MMI). MMI means no treatment will improve his or her medical condition.

Permanent partial disability (PPD) – The employee can return to his or her pre-injury employment but still has some level of physical or emotional impairment.

Permanent total disability (PTD) – The employee is unable to return to any meaningful employment. After this finding, the employee usually receives wage loss benefits for life.

Your adjuster will use these terms when discussing claims with you. These definitions should help you better understand the wage replacement in the claims process.

Comorbidities In Workers' Compensation A Troubling Trend For Insurers

Consider these two additional factors in preventing injuries: Injury frequency and injury severity. Injury frequency is the number of employees injured per month or year. Injury severity is the number of lost workdays for an injury once an injury occurs. For our purposes, we'll also consider the amount paid on a claim as part of severity.

While injury frequency in the United States has dropped in the past decade, injury severity is increasing. Increasing medical costs and issues of comorbidity are driving this increase. Comorbidities – preexisting medical conditions that aggravate a workplace injury – become an issue when an employee has pre-existing health conditions that can complicate healing.

Comorbidities are on the rise in the U.S. Here are just some we see in today's workforce.

- Alcohol or drug abuse
- Depression and anxiety
- Diabetes
- Hypertension
- Obesity

Any of these conditions can greatly increase claims payments. Adjusters and workers' compensation physicians work hard to determine which symptoms arise from the injury. They also try to determine which medical conditions preexist. These are often difficult to determine precisely. A report by the National Council on Compensation Insurance (NCCI) found that the number of workers' compensation claims that involved a comorbidity diagnosis almost tripled from accident years 2000 to 2009. Today, that number probably is much greater.

Another factor on the horizon that alarms workers' compensation executives is the aging of our workforce. An aging workforce impacts claim severity. In 2020, those 55 and older accounted for 36.4 percent of the U.S. workforce. Americans are increasingly working longer. A 2016 report from Stanford University found that 17 percent of Americans between ages 70 and 74 worked at least ten hours weekly.

The increasing age of our workforce may continue to impact medical costs. Older workers suffer fewer injuries. However, several studies found that older workers often incur significantly higher medical expenses. These studies cite two main reasons: increased time to heal and more work time missed.

According to the U.S. Bureau of Labor Statistics (BLS), older workers have high rates of slips, trips, and falls. Additionally, workers age 55 and older are more likely to suffer a fatal injury on the job, especially in farming occupations. This means investing in fall-reduction techniques can greatly reduce the cost of claims, such as better lighting and reducing clutter.

The fact that aging workers may have more serious injuries if they do get hurt should not encourage you to discriminate against older workers. They bring more benefits than risks to the workforce with their experience and maturity.

Today, both older and younger workers pose and will increasingly present significant challenges for insurance carriers.

Mental Health A Growing Challenge In Workers' Compensation Claims Management

Mental health issues are increasing in America. Mental health practitioners diagnose one in four adults in America with a mental disorder in any given year, according to John Hopkins Medicine. Any of these medical issues can complicate healing, thus affecting workers' compensation claims. Despite any challenges with mental health, employers cannot discriminate in hiring or providing medical treatment because an employee has a comorbidity.

Any injury and the subsequent absence from the workforce, coupled with the use of pain medication, can cause employees to become depressed. Therefore, returning employees to work as quickly as possible post-injury can help. We'll discuss this later in greater detail.

You cannot discuss an employee's health conditions in the interview process. Never make the mistake of asking potential employees about their medical conditions. This can lead you directly into employment litigation. We'll discuss pre-employment best practices in Chapter Five.

Aging workers and anxious employees are not today's only challenges. In 2014, the Wall Street Journal found that more than two-thirds of youth today would not qualify for service in the US military due to obesity, use of prescription medication for attention deficit disorder, appearance issues like tattoos, and felony convictions. Although employers have become increasingly tolerant of criminal backgrounds and tattoos, we must understand and embrace our younger workers. A recent study by the National Institute of Occupational Safety and Health found that workers between 16 and 25 were more risk-tolerant than their older coworkers.

Today's younger workforce wants more autonomy and may lack the cognitive maturity which develops later in life, leaving them more likely to get injured. These young men and women enter our workforce each day. We must train them and mentor them differently than older generations. Providing safety tips on mobile applications is just one way to accommodate the different learning styles of today's younger workforce.

As employers, we face a growing talent crisis. Construction companies sometimes take weeks or months to find the labor needed to fill vacancies and often hire casual labor to fill employment gaps. Casual labor can be a workers' compensation issue, even when hiring a temp worker from a reputable day-labor company. If you hire a temporary worker, be sure you obtain a certificate of insurance from the temp agency. This is no guarantee their insurer will cover the injured temporary worker, but it's a start.

Workforce Wellness More Important Now Than Ever

It pays to keep your employees healthy. Employees increasingly struggle with mental health issues, and work from home may add to that struggle. Increased isolation from coworkers can trigger depression. In one recent survey, 91 percent of Gen Z employees wanted a mental health policy in their workplace.

Employers must respond to societal trends, like it or not. This can include training employees to be prepared for and to prevent, when possible, workplace violence, another growing challenge for employers.

Financial problems can distract stressed employees, making them more error-prone, according to the Society for Human Resource Management. Consider instituting financial wellness training for your employees, as well. A study by Northwestern Mutual in 2019 found that one in five Baby Boomers have less than $5,000 savings for retirement.

Employers rely increasingly on telehealth, and many insurers have now turned to remote medical treatment for workers' compensation claims. While younger workers may embrace online appointments and communication through medical portals, more seasoned workers may struggle.

Growing Frequency And Severity Equal Higher Claims Costs

When your insurance carrier refers to injury frequency, this means how many injuries your workers have in a specific time period. Despite a decade-long decline perhaps due to better safety practices, injury frequency may again be on the rise in America. Injury severity – the lost workdays and the cost of a claim – is rising. Long waits for treatment due to COVID exacerbated this trend.

What can cause an increase in frequency? In a troubled economy, safety training is often the first casualty of budget cuts. Some experts believe fewer safety programs may be the problem. However, others think that employers hire less-experienced workers more cheaply than highly skilled workers idled since the pandemic hit. Less-experienced workers can increase the frequency of your workers' compensation claims.

Medical And Other Claims Costs Continue To Rise

Injury claims are becoming more costly to settle. No matter how well your adjusters manage the medical piece of your employee's injury, costs continue to rise. According to the NCCI, a variety of factors increase claims costs. These include more expensive wage replacement costs, higher partial and total disability awards when workers suffer permanent impairment, and soaring medical costs. Many workers' compensation experts predict that these costs, along with COVID-related factors, will force workers' compensation rates to rise. As these rates begin to climb nationally, one insurance brokerage forecasts that employers may suffer sticker shock.

One of the nation's largest insurance brokerages estimates that employers with more exposure to COVID-19 losses may face a surcharge from $0.01 to $0.24 per $100 of payroll. And COVID-19 challenges not only tested business owners' patience but caused many delays in medical treatment for injured workers. This increased lost wage payments and delayed return to work.

It is clear U.S. business owners face a difficult workers' compensation market.

What Can I Do As An Employer?

Between more frequent accidents and higher costs, what steps can you take to reduce losses and trim costs? You do not have to be an insurance expert to improve your workers' compensation program. The efforts outlined in this book do not have to cost much, and you will not need pricey experts to implement important organizational change. In just two hours, you can learn how savvy business owners improve their workers' compensation programs.

We explore practical actions you can implement or strengthen in your organization. These measures will help retool and improve your workers' compensation program. If you apply some or all these measures, you will reduce injury frequency, boost employee morale and attendance, and improve injury management if accidents do occur.

Each chapter will explore one of these actions. In less than the time it will take you to read this book, you can discover an entirely new model that will dramatically improve the way you manage your workers' compensation program.

As a former risk and claims manager, and an owner of a contracting company, I know first-hand how hard it is to manage risk. You'll miss your target if you take the shotgun approach to safety and expect to reduce losses. You must take the rifle approach – develop a detailed action plan, set a goal, aim, then shoot for your goal. Critical to this process is ensuring that if you do not meet your goal, you determine why and then fix that obstacle to goal mastery.

You must monitor the results of your efforts to ensure you are hitting the target each time. If not, how will your aim improve the next time you fire? This book will help you in most of the critical areas where business owners struggle when managing their workers' compensation program.

What's Next?

Here are the most important steps you can take to help prevent workers' compensation injuries in your organization. When an injury occurs to one of your employees, these suggestions will help ensure that you and your insurer respond rapidly. You'll learn some questions to ask your carrier to help ensure excellent claims management.

1. Find an agent or broker who understands your unique industry niche and who specializes in selling and servicing workers' compensation coverage.

2. Understand your insurance policy, which is a key compo-

nent in protecting your business assets.

3. Develop a strong safety culture led by top management, who sets the example. While managers must walk the safety talk, they must also enforce consequences for unsafe actions. A safety culture, which includes accountability for unsafe actions and behaviors, is critical to accident reduction.

4. Bulletproof your hiring practices. By using prescreening and pre-employment tools, you help prevent hiring mistakes. Your next workers' compensation claim may be sitting outside your company's human resources office as you read this, waiting for an interview.

5. Develop a comprehensive employee safety training program. Injuries occur more frequently to employees in their first months on a new job. New-hire safety orientations are critical. However, employees also need ongoing reminders and updated training throughout the year.

6. Train supervisors in accident investigation and safety oversight. Then, make sure they investigate each accident or injury.

7. Establish a loss prevention committee with the authority to make safety recommendations. Be sure to include at least a few line employees. They know the realities of what happens on the job site.

8. Report all injuries to your workers' compensation insurer within 24 hours. The longer you delay, the more the claim will cost and the more likely it is your employee will lose time from work or hire an attorney.

9. Develop strong relationships with your claims handlers, the front-line heroes who manage your employees' injuries. Their expertise and loyalty to your organization makes a critical difference in controlling your program costs.

10. Ensure your insurance carrier hires nurse case managers to keep more serious injuries moving forward. Also, consider a 24-

hour phone nursing service to triage all injuries. The cost of those services will more than pay for themselves.

11.   Institute a stay-at-work/return-to-work (SAW/RTW) program. Statistics show that injured workers who miss work for more than six weeks are much less likely to ever return to employment. Even one day of lost time hits your experience modification (emod) factor. Your emod is a critical factor used by insurance carriers to estimate your rates and your premiums and to account for your safety record. You'll find a detailed discussion of emods in Chapter Thirteen.

12.   Understand and manage your emod, a key factor in determining your premium. Your emod is the multiplier used by insurers to calculate your workers' compensation premium. Your emod is based on your claims experience compared to similar businesses in your class.

13.   Understand that your insurer will audit your premium each year. Audits rarely return premium. Know how to best prepare for and respond to the premium audit.

14.   Develop a feel for emerging risks that can impact your workers' compensation losses.

Let's next review the key parts of your workers' compensation insurance policy.

CHAPTER TWO - UNDERSTANDING YOUR WORKERS' COMPENSATION POLICY

As with any insurance policy, few business owners actually read their workers' compensation policy. While your agent can explain your policy in depth, let's cover the basics.

Does my business need workers' compensation coverage?

You may think, "I only have one employee. I don't need workers' compensation coverage." The state where you run your business determines the workers' compensation laws that apply to you. For example, if you're in Alaska, Colorado, or Arizona, one employee, even a part-time person, triggers the requirement for coverage. In fact, many states require coverage with only one full- or part-time employee. If you're uncertain about your state laws, go online to your state's workers' compensation division.

You may be a sole proprietor with no employees and think you don't need coverage. But do you have a family that you support? What happens if you can't work after a work-related auto accident? Loss of income from your business could ruin your finances. Workers' compensation coverage is available for solo business owners, even contractors. Most sole practitioners can benefit from workers' compensation insurance.

If you form a limited liability corporation (LLC), many states allow the business owners to opt out of coverage. However, the rates for owners of a company are usually pretty low, so why would you opt out? In today's era of distracted driving, one auto accident can easily disable you for a long time.

To better understand your coverage, let's review your workers' compensation policy sections.

Understanding Your Workers' Compensation Policy

Workers' compensation policies are probably the most standardized policies in insurance. A policy written in Georgia will look similar to one written in Missouri. The wording of workers' compensation policies is similar from state to state, as well.

Here are the usual policy sections.

Part One – Workers' Compensation Insurance

Part Two – Employers Liability Insurance

Part Three – Other States Insurance

Part Four – Your Duties if an Injury Occurs

Part Five – Premium

Part Six – Conditions

Let's review each policy section.

Your Information Page

Your Information Page is similar to the declarations sheet on other policies you purchase, like your property policy. Your Information Page describes the following.

- Your business name and type of operation, e.g., an LLC or partnership
- Your policy period
- Which states apply for coverage
- The employers' liability limit
- Your workforce classification codes, e.g., clerical 8810
- Your experience modification factor if you have one
- Your premium

Make sure that the policy correctly lists your job classifications and all states where your employees work, live or may travel for work, even rarely. In many cases, employees have the right to file a claim in the state where they live. If your remote employee lives in California and you operate in Arizona, the employee will probably choose the richer benefit state of California to adjudicate the injury.

As we noted in the introduction, failing to list a subsidiary business can mean you won't have the coverage you need should a claim occur.

Let's review each policy part.

Part One – Workers' Compensation Insurance

Workers' compensation is a liability policy. Part One lists the benefits to your injured employees. However, unlike your general liability coverage, Part One does not set a dollar limit. The state where you operate dictates amounts payable. This means the insurer will pay any benefits according to state-mandated amounts if your worker suffers an injury. Your insurer and the state workers' compensation statutes determine how much the insurer pays for that employee's medical bills, lost wages, and any permanent benefits. The injured worker or his or her attorney agrees to settlement amounts if disputed.

Part One states the insurer will pay any benefits owed for an industrial injury or illness as required by the states listed in Part Three of the policy. Any loss must occur during the policy period listed on the information page.

Part Two – Employers Liability Insurance

An employee may make a claim for an injury that your policy does not cover due to your state's workers' compensation laws. If this happens, Part Two may protect you. Remember that grand bargain? An injured worker waives his or her right to sue the employer in exchange for medical care, lost wages, rehabilitation, and other statutory benefits.

There are exceptions. Here are a few examples of occurrences that can create liability.

- Your employee feels that you were negligent, usually beyond simple negligence. For example, suppose employees complain about a lack of safety guards on a crushing machine. Your supervisors modify and then finally remove those guards. Your employee loses a hand in the machine. This could prompt a claim against you, an employer's liability claim.

- Your employee's family seeks compensation for the loss of their family member or for having to care for that family member after a serious illness or injury.

- You manufacture a product, and the product injures your employee. This is known as dual capacity because you are both the manufacturer and the employer.

Employers' liability claims can also arise if your employee sues a manufacturer after his or her injury. In the case of the crushing machine, your employee may sue the machine manufacturer. The manufacturer in turn sues you for your alleged negligence in modifying their machine. These are known as third-party over-claims.

This policy section lists a liability limit. The basic limit is usually $100,000 per accident, $500,000 per policy, and $100,000 per employee. Depending on your operation and contractual requests for projects you may perform, you may need higher limits. Your agent can provide quotes at various levels.

Part Three – Other States Insurance

If you expand your operations into states other than those listed on your information page, you must obtain coverage in that state. Additionally, if your employees travel to or live in other states, you need coverage in those states.

Often your insurer operates in most states and may protect you in those states with wording in this provision. However, if you operate in a monopolistic state, your agent can help you procure coverage in that state directly from the state agency. The monopolistic states are North Dakota, Ohio, Washington and Wyoming, Puerto Rico, and the U.S. Virgin Islands. Also, your general liability insurer may offer stop-gap coverage. If you operate at any level in monopolistic states, do not go without coverage. Here's a key rule of risk management – Do not risk a lot to save a little.

Part Four – Your Duties If An Injury Occurs

Like any policy you purchase, workers' compensation is a contract that requires both parties to comply with its conditions. Many of them are common sense, such as providing your employees with immediate medical care post-injury. Some conditions also can cause problems. Examples are failing to cooperate with your insurer after a loss or failure to preserve evidence after an injury. If someone else is at fault, your insurer will want to subrogate to collect any monies owed for their payments.

Even if you contributed to an injury, such as modifying a machine, you must preserve the evidence for your insurer. This is true even if you know that evidence will work against you.

Part Five – Premium

This part of the policy defines how the insurer calculates your premium. It will include

- the rules your insurer uses,
- your job classifications, codes the insurer uses to set rates,
- your anticipated payroll levels per class code,
- your "rate per $100 of remuneration" [payroll], and
- your estimated annual premium.

When you apply for or renew coverage, you estimate your payroll. This estimate can definitely change at year-end, as we'll explain later in this book. Class codes, too, can cause problems, which we'll discuss.

Here is an issue we found in our plumbing business. We consider our senior plumber a manager because he provides estimates and oversees the less-experienced plumbers. At audit, after I described his duties to our auditor, he did not agree. He changed his class code from a supervisor class code to a plumbing class code. This revision generated an additional premium because the manager class code is a lower rate per hundred of payroll than is the plumbing code.

You may have an employee who changes job duties during the policy period. In that case, you'll want to estimate his or her payroll for each class code.

Most auditors will discuss class code changes with you if you contact them. You can debate their decisions. It's fun, but it's not a lot of fun. However, rest assured that in many cases, you won't win. If you have questions on class codes, have your agent get an agreement with your underwriter first. This is better than waiting for an audit and an almost certain additional premium.

Part Six – Conditions

This section defines the rights and obligations of both parties to the insurance contract. These can include the following.

Inspection – Your insurer can inspect your workplace to determine workforce conditions. Not only that, but at audit, your auditor can check relevant records to verify your payroll and class codes.

Transfer of the policy – You cannot transfer this policy to a new owner. Your insurer will re-underwrite the policy after any ownership changes.

Cancellation – Unless state statutes apply, your insurer must give at least ten days' notice prior to cancellation. You must also provide advance notice of cancellation. However, no set number of days' notice prior to cancellation applies to the policyholder.

Sole representation –Your policy may name more than one insured. However, only the first-named insured has all rights to act on the conditions of the policy and on behalf of all insureds. This includes payments, refunds, and cancellations, to name a few items.

"I 1099 All My Workers; They're Not Employees."

Making a mistake in obtaining workers' compensation coverage or failing to obtain coverage when needed can be a big problem for today's business owners. Many, many contractors I've talked to think because they "1099" their workers, these workers are not employees. Therefore, they do not buy workers' compensation coverage. If your state's industrial commission defines your 1099 worker as an employee, what happens?

First, you lose the protection of the Grand Bargain. Your 1099 employee may be able to file suit against you. Next, the state may begin to pay benefits from a special fund for non-insured workers.

As we'll discuss later, judges who administer the state compensation laws dislike seeing workers burdened by medical bills and other injury losses if there is any chance they are employees, rather than independent contractors. Finally, once the state settles your employee's claim, they'll come looking to you for repayment.

You will not find the needed coverage for an injured employee under your general liability policy, either. Insurers design insurance policies so that they dovetail to avoid duplicating coverage. Your liability policy specifically excludes coverage for liabilities that arise under workers' compensation laws.

Generally, to determine if an employee is indeed an independent contractor, adjusters review the Internal Revenue Service (IRS) definitions. Three common rules are as follows.

Behavioral – Do you control what the worker does and how s/he does that job? This can include what time s/he does the job, for example.

Financial – Who provides your workers' tools, supplies, etc.

Type of relationship – Do you have a written contract or provide health or liability insurance for your worker?

If in doubt, the IRS suggests you file a Form SS-8, which outlines the duties your workers perform. However, the IRS warns it takes about six months to get a determination. When in doubt, contact a labor attorney or your local trade association. Don't be blindsided by all the problems connected to classifying employees as independent contractors if they are not.

Next, let's discuss how to find the best agent for your business.

CHAPTER THREE - WHETHER AGENT OR BROKER, LOOK FOR THE BEST

Do you work with an insurance agent or broker who thoroughly understands your industry? As your organization has grown and diversified, has your agent grown with you? Does your agent provide excellent customer service not only at renewal time but throughout the year? Does he or she add value to your organization? If the only time you see your agent is just prior to renewal, you may need a new agent.

How do you know if your insurance agent or broker, as well as your insurance coverage, is right for you?

Passing The Insurance Exam Is Just The Beginning

I am never surprised when I tell people that I am in the insurance industry and they respond, "I used to be an insurance agent!" Sometimes they are my waitperson in a restaurant, selling hot tubs, or pitching some other commodity. You can easily find hundreds of thousands of licensed insurance agents and formerly licensed ones. Passing the licensing exam, administered on a state-by-state basis, is not hard. Passing the exam is the first small sum in the equation of an insurance agent's professional development, however.

Purchasing the right workers' compensation coverage for your business and properly structuring your program are critical elements in your business solvency. Choosing an agent or insurance broker who understands your unique business demands is vitally important to your business success.

Agents and brokers vary greatly by industry. For example, claim severity in the construction industry is about 50 percent higher than for all other industries combined. If you are a contractor, you need an agent who understands the unique risks you face daily. If you operate a home care agency, the same applies. In fact, you need such an agent no matter what your business.

Agent Or Broker?

A multinational company's needs are much more involved than those of a small manufacturer or a plumbing company with only a handful of employees. One of the first questions you should ask is, "Do I need an insurance agent or a broker?" Which you choose depends on the complexity of your business.

Typically, an agent acts as an "authorized agent" of the insurance company. In a sense, an agent works for an insurance company. An agent presents your organization's insurance profile to several insurers who write the type of business you run. They usually earn a fixed percentage of your premium when placing your coverage.

On the other hand, a broker works for and represents you. Brokers usually approach many insurers on your behalf. They may write your insurance on a fee-for-service basis or a flat fee. Brokers typically have access to many different insurance markets and often hire brokers who specialize in particular lines of coverage, like aviation or professional liability.

Some insurance agents and brokers (also called insurance producers) accept contingency commissions. Contingency commissions are profit-sharing agreements between an agent or broker and the insurance company. This commission is an incentive to the agent or broker for the placement of profitable accounts with that insurer. For example, let's say Insurer X writes an account at a $100,000 annual premium and pays only $63,000 in claims for that policy period. The underwriting profit on that account is much higher than a $100,000 account that generates $220,000 in claims.

Insurers use contingencies to motivate agents and brokers to submit business to them that offers a high likelihood of profitability. Most agents disclose contingency commissions, but not all do. Most agents and brokers are ethical and honest. Do your due diligence, however, and insist that your agent or broker provide the proposals offered by all the companies they approach for you. Also ask your agent to divulge any fees and commissions, especially if they work for you on a fee-for-service basis. This helps you evaluate their worth to your organization. For example, you may pay an annual fixed fee-for-service, but that fee includes 40 hours of loss prevention services. This helps you avoid hiring a consultant to fix a problem that your agent or broker is capable of solving with you.

Whether you use a broker or an agent, you should receive the same service – the marketing of your company to carefully selected insurance carriers. Further, you should receive prompt follow-up support if claims or questions arise.

Your agent should analyze the various coverage forms, negotiate discounts, add coverage enhancements when available, and negotiate premium credits on your behalf. At the end of this period of analyzing and negotiating on your behalf, your agent or broker should help you decide which company you want to be insured with. Remember, though, the decision you make on which insurer you choose is yours, not your agent's or your broker's. They can guide you, but ultimately if you don't understand what you're buying, ask for more information before you decide.

Choose An Agent Who Really Knows The Workers'

Compensation Market

The reality today is that some workers' compensation carriers are leaving the market and others are raising rates as the workers' compensation market tightens. Insurance professionals call this a "hard" insurance market.

Finding a good agent is not easy. According to a recent article in Insurance Journal, one in seven agents will have an errors and omissions claim filed against them in a year's time. How do you find that agent who can provide access to the best markets? How can you find that agent who can add value to your business by helping you reduce claims and lower your emod, which impacts your premium? What makes an outstanding agent?

First, look for an agent with a professional designation, like the Chartered Property Casualty Underwriter (CPCU), which is the gold standard for commercial property/casualty agents. The Certified Insurance Counselor (CIC) is also a solid designation for agents. Both designations require ongoing training and adherence to a strict set of ethical standards. In addition to designations, ask how long your agent has been in business, what professional organizations s/he joins, and what references can s/he provide from clients in industries similar to yours, if possible.

Kevin Quinley, an insurance claim expert and owner of Quinley Risk Associates in Chesterfield, Virginia, recommends that you "Pick an insurance agent who speaks plain English and not insurance-ese. If they prattle on about `mods' and use acronyms they presume that you know, that is a red flag."

You shouldn't need subtitles to understand your agent, Quinley believes. Good agents don't just sell or push insurance; they translate insurance concepts into plain English. A good agent or broker also checks in with you periodically to assess your needs and degree of satisfaction, not just at renewal time to sell you more products.

"Find an agent who is familiar with your class of business

and really understands your unique environment, challenges and needs," Quinley said. "Go for the agent's or broker's experience over promises."

Several Ways To Find Good Agents

One of the best ways to find good agents is through the national association, The Independent Insurance Agents & Brokers of America, the "Big I." Agents and brokers who join this nationwide organization represent some of the finest insurance companies in the world. Through their Trusted Choice brand, you can find a local agent or broker who specializes in workers' compensation coverage. If you'd like to call, contact the Big I association in your state. Representatives from the Big I can discuss your business scope and the coverages you seek and refer you to an agent or broker who can assist you.

Fair warning – Only a small percentage of agents specialize in workers' compensation coverage. Another place to find agents who are highly training in managing workers' compensation insurance is ReSource Pro. ReSource Pro acquired Oceanus Partners, founded in 2009 by Frank Pennachio and Susan Toussaint. Today ReSource Pro is a premier industry group that trains agents to specialize in writing workers' compensation coverage.

These agents receive high-level guidance that prepares them to advocate for their policyholders. ReSource Pro-trained agents are specially qualified to provide a thorough analysis of your emod. They can help you ensure reserves are correct before they can negatively impact your emod and help you better manage claims if they do occur. I attended a rigorous three-day training with agents in this network, many attending for their second or third time. This type of well-trained agent adds value to their clients.

One caveat. If your premium generates less than about $2,500 in commission, you may have a tough time finding an agent to work closely with you. Experienced agents are usually busy and specialize in one or more industry niches. There are scores of younger, very smart agents entering the insurance industry. They will be more willing to work with you.

Choosing an agent is not always easy. Some larger organizations use a process managed by an independent consultant, who reviews insurance proposals and provides coverage advice. If you run a smaller company, you must rely heavily on referrals from business associates, ideally those in your industry. Industry trade groups can provide strong agent referrals, as well.

Your Relationship With Your Agent Is Critical To Your Fiscal Solvency

The public trusts independent insurance agents almost 50 percent more than banks and 97 percent more than health carriers, according to a survey commissioned by The Hanover Insurance Group. This survey consisted of 501 small businesses with fewer than 30 employees each. The respondents rated "trust" as the key factor in choosing an agent. Finding an experienced agent or broker you can trust is critical to your business's success.

Your agent should understand the unique challenges you face each day you open your doors. Find an agent who knows your industry and specializes in selling and servicing workers' compensation coverage. He or she should also understand how to interpret your emod factors. The agent should talk to your claims adjusters when claim issues arise and be able to assist you with your yearly premium audit, which we'll discuss in more depth later.

A carefully chosen broker or agent can help you reduce your risks while helping to ensure you are adequately insured. They should be your solid resource when risk management issues arise.

Now let's look at how building a proper safety culture can improve your organization and help you manage your workers' compensation program.

CHAPTER FOUR - REDUCE LOSSES WITH A STRONG SAFETY CULTURE

When building your workers' compensation program, your first task may be the most critical to reducing accidents and injuries. That task is building a strong safety culture. Your management team builds safer workplaces when they create an atmosphere that says, day in and day out, "We value you, so safety first. We want every employee to go home whole at the end of each shift."

Few employees will lead the way to safety; they wait for their bosses to set the example. To reduce accidents and prevent injuries, a company's management team must model and mold values, behaviors, attitudes, and practices that promote safety. However, a safety culture requires more than just managers talking the safety talk. Management must infuse safety into every meeting. Further, they must investigate every mishap with a clear message – we put safety before profits. Managers must furnish the tools employees need to work safely. Additionally, your employees must understand that consequences always follow unsafe actions, a critical element in accident reduction.

These are the most important actions company officials can take to build a strong safety culture.

The management team must model and support safe behavior

Astute managers consistently model, remind and support the significance of safety in their organization. Managers and supervisors should display the behavior they expect employees to practice. If supervisors or managers take shortcuts, for example, failing to lock out electrical equipment for small repair jobs, so will your employees. Managers must remind employees that no task, large or small, is worth the risk of an injury. No matter the employee's role in the organization, each worker is a valued resource who deserves to go home safely.

Catch an employee doing something right

When we ask employees in tough times to do more with fewer workers and when raises and bonuses are scarce, appreciation and recognition are more important than ever. Today's employees increasingly jump from employer to employer, making retaining employees in a tough job market more important than ever.

It is often easier to criticize than to praise. However, frequent criticism can backfire. Instead, watch for employees who model safe behavior and apply liberal praise. Praising performance makes workers feel appreciated and builds confidence. When an employee "does something right," reinforcing that correct behavior will help you build a safer culture.

Training should be systematic and timely

Budgeting is key to profitability. When stretched, organizations frequently eliminate training to reduce costs. Yet as layoffs trim ranks and businesses eliminate highly experienced workers, training becomes more essential than ever.

According to the BLS, Monday is the most frequent day for a workplace injury. When we consider injury red flags, Monday-morning injuries are one indicator of possible fraud. However, a sedentary weekend followed by exertion on Monday can also explain a Monday injury.

Additionally, older workers have fewer injuries. Younger employees typically work irregular hours or perform more strenuous manual tasks.

English As A Second Language Challenges

There are special challenges for employees who speak English as a second language. According to the Center for Immigration Studies, in 2018 more than 67.3 million U.S. residents spoke a foreign language at home. Non-native speakers sometimes say they understand, but they may not fully grasp the task. Making matters worse, they may feel uncomfortable asking questions.

One plumbing contractor we know was relining a sewer pipe in a whole-home sewer improvement. His Spanish-speaking employee was in the bathroom on one end as the contractor injected the liner into the bathroom. His employee assured the contractor he knew which pipe to use but fed the liner into the wrong pipe. Fixing it involved jackhammering up the customer's floor and replacing the toilet, the tile, and trim, not to mention the time spent smoothing the customer's irritation. Taking an extra moment to ensure that his worker understood his instructions by pointing out the correct pipe would have meant a larger profit on the job. One communication failure can equal an angry customer and a job with no profit, not to mention a severe injury.

Nor can we assume that new hires received enough training in their prior positions. We cannot assume employees know even the fundamentals of operating equipment safely. Invest in initial training and reinforce safe behaviors. These two measures help keep employees injury-free and generate a stronger return on investment.

If you're hiring a service technician, for example, have the new tech ride with an experienced technician for a week or so. The experienced tech can watch the new tech's driving habits, installation skills, and probably most importantly, the tech's customer service skills. Many look good on paper but don't always perform well.

One of the largest plumbing contractors in the Bay Area said he hires used car salesmen and trains them to plumb. He said, "Even if they flood a customer's house, customers will use us again because they like the employee."

Ensuring applicants have excellent customer service skills should be a company's first priority when hiring.

Could You Snack On Your Shop Floor?

Good housekeeping and appropriate maintenance should define your organization. When they inspect facilities, OSHA inspectors notice poor housekeeping and shoddy maintenance. As one loss prevention professional said, "The first thing I look for is good housekeeping. Your attitude toward housekeeping is a direct reflection of your attitude toward safety."

A dirty and disorganized worksite hurts morale. Disarray also increases the chance that OSHA officials will stay longer and dig deeper while on site. Keep inspectors moving through your facility and boost employee morale by keeping work areas spotless, well-organized, and well-maintained.

A Safety Culture Encourages Employees To Take Time To Work Safely

Cutting corners to save time inevitably causes serious injuries. Time constraints are never an excuse to bypass safe procedures. Your company should clearly communicate and reinforce this message to all employees from your new hires to the most seasoned worker.

Involve Front-Line Employees In Safety Processes

Making important decisions without input from your line employees can be a mistake. Your front-line employees and supervisors best understand realities on the shop floor and in the field. They are your problem solvers, the ones who can take a complex problem and creatively solve it, often without any help from managers or supervisors.

Your line employees must feel free to report problems, near misses, and malfunctions with no fear of negative consequences. It is a manager's job to ask, "What tools do you need to do the job?" Providing resources and general direction are key roles of management.

If workers report smaller problems and you as a manager or supervisor correct them, your organization can avoid big problems and injuries. If employees feel safe and appreciated, they will feel comfortable offering input into processes and procedures. Ignoring or ridiculing employee suggestions shuts down creativity and builds resentment. These deficits ultimately cost your company by reducing innovation and increasing operational problems.

Does Your Organization Encourage Safe Behavior?

Tying safe behaviors to salary increases and promotions is critically important to your safety culture. Safety awards encourage and improve safe behaviors. While experts recommend team awards over individual awards, small items like patches that reward safe driving and callouts in team meetings for safe practices can improve morale and keep safety forefront in employees' minds.

In larger organizations, cost allocation fairly distributes insurance costs to departments based on that department's loss experience. A cost-allocation program encourages departments to consider safety in every decision they make. This is a simple and incomplete explanation of cost-allocation programs. Developing a cost-allocation program is beyond the scope of this book. However, you can work with a risk management consultant or your insurer to develop and implement this important program for your business.

Ignoring unsafe behavior sends the wrong message to employees. Employers reinforce a safety culture when they hold all employees accountable, including management. Organizational culture always begins and ends with top management. As Peter Drucker said, "Culture eats strategy for breakfast."

Ensuring your employees follow safety protocols are critical to reshaping unsafe behaviors. Any investments you make in your organization's safety culture will help decrease accidents and boost your profits.

Next, let's consider how improved employment practices will help you avoid hiring your next workers' compensation claim.

CHAPTER FIVE - BETTER HIRING PRACTICES REDUCE INJURIES AND INCREASE YOUR PROFITS

I've heard many risk managers say, "Your next workers' compensation injury is sitting outside your human resources department right now, waiting for an interview." I've also heard repeatedly from supervisors when an employee has a questionable workers' compensation injury, "I should have fired him/her months ago."

Solid hiring and retention practices will help prevent injuries. Systematic prescreening and pre-employment physicals help prevent costly hiring mistakes.

We Take Our Employees As We Find Them

Clichés develop because they are true. One of the first truths adjusters learn when they begin handling workers' compensation claims is that "We take employees as we find them." This means that whether we hire employees with medical issues or employees develop medical problems after hire, we may pay for complications in injuries that happen at work. For example, a diabetes diagnosis can mean impaired lower limb function. A toe blister can result in an amputation. Would that amputation have occurred minus diabetes? Undoubtedly, no. However, in most instances, the insurer will pay for the amputation, the disfigurement, if any, and the resulting wage loss.

Employers cannot discriminate against employees with prior injuries or medical conditions if they can perform the job's essential functions. Essential functions are the job duties the employee must perform either with or without reasonable accommodation, according to the U.S. Equal Employment Opportunity Commission (EEOC). A thorough pre-employment physical can help you establish if your potential hire can perform the prospective job's essential functions. Your job description should spell out those functions before you advertise for the job.

Pre-Employment Physicals Are Not All Alike

Not all pre-employment physicals are helpful, however. Many physical examinations will not uncover the issues that can cause an employee injury. Pre-employment physicals are often little more than a doctor chatting with a patient and checking boxes on a form. Many are cursory examinations that determine little more than if an employee is breathing and whether his or her current blood pressure and weight fall in the normal range. But to determine whether an employee can actually perform the essential functions of a job, that physical must be thorough. Either a physician or a physical therapist trained to evaluate physical abilities needed to safely complete job tasks should complete the physical. These tests can include muscular tension tests, endurance tests, cardiovascular endurance tests, and flexibility and balance tests.

Schedule the examination only after you extend a written conditional employment offer. If your employees must have an acceptable driving record, an acceptable criminal background, or pass a drug screen, outline these conditions in the letter, as well.

Many physicians fail to obtain a thorough medical history or perform a detailed physical examination. Find a few occupational physicians who specialize in pre-employment physicals. They usually obtain a detailed health history. This approach can uncover problems that could later lead to a workplace injury. Limit the medical history only to health information that can impact the ability to carry out the job's essential functions.

Some organizations do not want the entire examination results. They want the examining physician to indicate whether the potential hire can complete the job's essential functions. If you do receive the medical information, federal law requires that you file it separately from the personnel file.

Consistency Is Key

If you conduct pre-employment examinations, be consistent. If you hire two warehouse workers, for example, either perform examinations for both or neither to avoid discrimination charges. If your applicants' medical conditions prevent their employment, their elimination must be "job-related and justified by business necessity," according to the EEOC. The cost to provide accommodation in the workplace is generally low. The Job Accommodation Network in one study found that a typical accommodation, such as an ergonomic keyboard, costs an organization $500 or less.

When your physician's opinion states the employee cannot safely perform the essential functions of the position, your applicant may challenge that with another doctor's opinion. If the applicant's physician offers a dissenting opinion, you may need a third opinion, usually paid by your company. When this occurs, work closely with a human resources consultant or legal counsel to avoid violating labor laws. Failure to comply with the Americans with Disabilities Act (ADA) can cost companies a great deal of administrative time and money in legal expenses.

Handled correctly, these exams can help to protect your organization against accusations of hiring discrimination.

Behavioral Testing Can Prevent Hiring Mistakes

You may not want to stop at physical examinations, however. Your employment physicals may include cognitive tests and mental status assessments. Tread carefully, however. Behavioral exams should relate to the job the applicant will perform. They should not wander into "nice to have" attributes.

Many organizations today implement pre-employment behavioral testing. These are often online tests designed to reveal character traits. Applicants answer questions designed to uncover whether they have lied or stolen in previous positions or if they are likely to resist return-to-work efforts.

Why would people answer questions about their character honestly? Because they may have rationalized their behavior, according to one employment expert. If they don't answer honestly, they may experience cognitive dissonance, an anxiety-provoking state where behaviors are in conflict with values.

These tests can establish more than whether an employee is likely to lie and steal. They help to determine predictors of entitlement mentality, a trait that makes people more likely to steal and fake injuries. These employees may also behave in a riskier manner. These tests typically discover character traits, including the following, according to the Society for Human Resources.

- Conscientiousness
- Sociability
- Introversion versus extroversion
- Emotional stability and maturity
- Openness to new ideas

Positive association with these traits can predict better work behaviors. When we keep the potentially most troublesome applicants off the payroll, the reduction in workers' compensation losses is highly predictable. Selecting a new hire is more rational when you use testing that evaluates the applicant's level of integrity.

Pre-employment practices can be fertile ground for litigation with the expanded scope of the ADA and other federal regulations. If in doubt, hire legal counsel or a human resource consultant to assist you with these employment issues. Many human resource consultants work on a flat fee-for-service; others work on a retainer basis. Your payroll company may offer employment consulting services, usually for an additional cost.

Next, let's review the importance of safety training for both new and existing employees.

CHAPTER SIX - SAFETY TRAINING A KEY COMPONENT IN A SAFER WORKPLACE

An investment in employee training is one of the best ways to prevent injuries and reduce your workers' compensation premiums. A thoroughly planned and comprehensive employee training program will pay a healthy return on investment. Employers who consistently invest in training experience fewer injuries, boost morale and increase productivity.

No business owner is happy to hear the word "OSHA," especially if that OSHA official is on their doorstep. Although OSHA's current role stresses enforcement, it also provides consulting services to businesses throughout the United States. In many states, OSHA offers free safety training for small businesses and in some cases, partners with universities to offer highly specialized and inexpensive training. Take advantage of any free training OSHA offers to reduce your program costs. Contact your local state or federal OSHA office to learn when their training occurs.

A safety program should have the following five objectives.

1. Ensure your employees always come to a safe workplace that is free from avoidable hazards.

2. Provide thorough training on your company's rules, re-

sponsibilities, and procedures to ensure your employees work safely.

3. Make sure your company complies with all state and federal safety laws and document that compliance.

4. Provide your employees with easily accessible safety guidelines and thoroughly train personnel exposed to workplace hazards according to those guidelines.

5. Make sure employees understand that they are responsible to work safely. However, you must make it as easy as possible for them to do this. This means furnishing appropriate equipment and maintaining tools and machinery.

Ensure you train employees who perform both routine tasks such as driving and hazardous functions, such as electrical repairs.

Your safety program must not only protect your employees but also visitors and contractors working on your site.

Senior Management Leads The Safety Effort By Instituting The Safety Culture

No safety training program succeeds without management support. Your role as a business owner or manager is to provide administrative and financial assistance to ensure workers can and do perform their jobs safely.

Don't develop safety training in a vacuum. Seek input from frontline supervisors, who oversee workers and provide day-to-day operational oversight. They are your "boots on the ground." Frontline supervisors know the realities of the field and the shortcuts employees take to get the job done. They know first-hand how those shortcuts can have devastating consequences.

Taking a cookie-cutter training program and modifying it to your industry or workforce can almost guarantee failure. What works for General Motors with 155,000 employees in 2020 probably won't work for General Construction, a 20-person outfit.

Training is essential to the success of any organization. According to Georgia Tech safety specialists, injuries occur to employees most frequently in their first two years on the job or after they have been on the job for more than ten years. Training employees only when first hired does not make a safe workplace. Ongoing training is critical to safe operations. It gives employees the tools they need to succeed safely.

Basic Safety Principles For Every Organization

Georgia tech presenters outlined basic safety principles applicable to all jobs.

- Assess workers' abilities before they begin the task, not after they get hurt.
- Expect unexpected events.
- Identify hazards.
- Isolate equipment whenever possible. For example, when doing routine maintenance on a water heater, make sure you've turned off the electricity to the device and locked access to avoid a shock injury.
- Plan every job.
- Reduce hazards using engineering controls such as electrical lockout/tagout, if possible.
- Use state-of-the-art safety equipment to protect employees.
- Use personal protective equipment.
- Use the right tools for the task.
- Use proper procedures learned at employee training and reminder tools, such as checklists for various tasks.

Consider the use of checklists, even for routine tasks. If checklists work for pilots and doctors, why wouldn't they work for your employees? Your employees can perform even routine tasks more safely with the use of properly created checklists. According to Atul Gawande, author of The Checklist Manifesto, checklists protect against failure.

Don't Threaten Employees With Osha Violations

I have attended or hired many safety trainers only to hear safety professionals warn employees of the dangers of an OSHA visit or citation. If they're my employees, I do damage control after they speak. I remind them, "It's management's job to worry about OSHA. We're holding this training because we want you, the employees, to go home free of injury to your families each day. That should be your focus." That sentiment speaks volumes to employees.

Never allow your trainers to use OSHA as a hammer. OSHA is there to protect workers. It's management's job to ensure compliance with OSHA regulations and to manage OSHA inspections.

Audit Workforce Activities For Continuous Improvement

Protecting your workforce should be one of every organization's primary goals. Developing adequate procedures, training to those procedures, and debriefing after a near miss may mean the difference between a day without an injury and one with a severe injury or a fatality. Adequate and ongoing training can ensure employees go home to their families each day.

Next, let's review the importance of thorough post-accident investigations.

CHAPTER SEVEN - INVESTIGATING ACCIDENTS AND NEAR-MISSES CAN HELP PREVENT RECURRENCES

Thoroughly training supervisors and managers to investigate incidents, even near misses, is a key element in preventing losses and reducing premiums.

When organizations perform thorough post-incident investigations, they profit from fewer claims as well as improved productivity. "Organizations with a strong safety focus know they must meticulously track both losses and near misses," according to Quinley. "Near misses and post-loss 'postmortems' provide important sources of 'intel'. They are weathervanes, pointing to areas of potential losses."

Savvy organizations analyze near misses to discern accident trends, identify root causes, formulate correction plans to attack those causes, execute plans, and monitor for results. Capturing data on near misses, analyzing the data, and developing proactive plans can prevent near misses from developing into accidents,

Quinley states.

A properly conducted investigation is the crux of compensability in workers' compensation claims. Your insurance carrier receives the first report of injury sometimes days after the incident occurs, often losing the opportunity to complete a scene investigation.

This is where the supervisor's investigation is critical. "Taking immediate scene photos and preserving evidence that may be crucial in subrogation is an important first step," Quinley continued.

Rely On Your Insurer For Loss Prevention Assistance

Take advantage of any loss prevention services your insurer offers. Some organizations shy away from asking their insurance carrier for help. Many companies either do not know about the services their insurance company offers or are afraid to ask for help.

Here's what Quinley had to say about this fact. "Some employers may have organizational hubris, thinking they don't have a problem or that they don't need insurer loss prevention intervention for worker safety."

Some organizations may be unaware of the loss control services available in workers' compensation. Others are wary of having an insurer's representative nose around their operations, fearing they will uncover some fact the carrier may seize upon to raise rates. Others may not see the value added to having an insurer come in or are skeptical that the insurer has experts that can help them, according to Quinley.

Most workers' compensation insurers have a wealth of expertise on board. They may have experts in setting up SAW/RTW programs, facility management, or fleet safety. Fleet safety programs are especially important in times of escalating auto claims, like now. No matter what your organization needs, your agent or insurer can build those services into your premiums. Take advantage of their loss prevention expertise. You will reduce your losses and save your company money. I guarantee you, loss prevention professionals never come in with a "gotcha" attitude. They're professionals who pride themselves on assisting your organization to keep employees safe.

Your insurer can help with regulatory compliance, as well. The first thing OSHA inspectors will request when they visit your facility is your hazard communication program. Your insurer can help you develop one and help train your supervisors in its use.

Even when timely reported, your insurance carrier investigates only a small number of your injuries. Medical-only claims receive minimum contact. Thoroughly investigating each injury is critical because even a minor hurt like a back strain can morph into a major injury. Once that progression occurs, it is often too late to investigate and change a compensability decision to a denial.

The Root Causes Of Incidents

Many safety experts agree that often several root causes or factors contribute to an incident. However, your task in an investigation is to identify as many as possible.

First, make sure you know exactly how the incident occurred. Then consider these factors when you investigate the incident.

- Machinery or materials failure; unsafe or defective equipment
- Prevention (actions management or supervisors can take to prevent recurrence)
- Proper supervision
- Task procedures (appropriate and pre-planned steps to safely complete the task)
- Training (lack of training, infrequent training, and trainer quality)

- Unsafe working conditions (poor housekeeping or incorrect footwear, for example, are often factors in slips and falls)

Your employees' attitudes and overall wellness are just as critical to safety as safe practices. Personal factors can cause injuries. Consider these crucial elements during your investigation.

- Consider the employee's physical ability to perform the essential job functions. Many times, an employee's physical condition deteriorates over time. The employee may no longer be able to complete all the essential functions of the job. These are tough cases, but if you don't act and consider the ADA implications, you can have a seriously injured employee and a big legal headache.

- Does the employee have a "beef" with the supervisor? Many organizations refuse to transfer employees to a different supervisor when there's a personality conflict. That is a rigid attitude few businesses can afford in today's workplace.

- Evaluate the employee's mental attitude. Were his or her work practices sloppy? Did the supervisor intervene in prior instances?

- Is overall morale low in the employee's unit? In this case, supervisors and managers may need reevaluation.

That's A Lot! Where Do We Start?

How do organizations prepare for their own accident investigations? Train all supervisors in accident investigation. Team new supervisors with more experienced managers who can teach them investigative techniques. Then, once trained, coach new investigators through the first few reviews they complete.

If you lack in-house expertise, you can send managers and supervisors to accident investigation training. Training your managers and supervisors to investigate accidents can help prevent recurrences and reduce losses. Employees work more safely if they know an injury is an organizational big deal.

If your budget lacks training funds, find free training. The Washington State Department of Labor and Industries offers a free online presentation, "Accident Investigation Basics," designed to train supervisors.

Many organizations rely heavily on their insurance companies to complete investigations after an injury. However, when employers investigate their own incidents then take steps to prevent recurrences, they can reduce compensable claims and decrease their organization's total cost of risk, sometimes by a substantial amount.

A simple policy like a "no-backing" rule in your fleet policy can dramatically decrease auto accidents and injuries. According to a recent article in the *National Underwriter*, distracted driving caused 74 percent of on-the-job vehicle accidents. Focusing on preventing distracted driving and a no-cell phone policy can help dramatically. As one large trucking firm owner in Arizona often reminds his drivers, "We're only one nuclear verdict away from bankruptcy."

These policies only work when reinforced.

The Five Whys Of Accident Investigation

Using "The Five Whys" is a straightforward way to get to the heart of accident causation. Developed by Sakichi Toyoda, the founder of Toyota Industries, The Five Whys is a solid investigation technique that helps you prevent similar incidents. If your company's accidents seem to recur in slightly different forms, maybe it is time to look again at your accident investigation techniques.

Analyzing the root cause of an accident is the basis of any accident investigation. What really caused the accident? The Five Whys lets even an inexperienced supervisor determine the root cause of an accident. Rather than revealing symptoms of an event, root-cause analysis determines the primary cause. Once you know an incident's root cause, you can correct that unsafe act or condition and prevent similar incidents.

The Five Whys shows your organization how to refocus resources to fix both personnel and equipment problems. Problems left untreated will recur.

How The Five Whys Works

Suppose one of your employees slips on a puddle in your shop's basement, falls, and breaks his arm. An easy fix would be to ensure someone cleans up the water, your employee receives appropriate medical treatment, and the workday continues. But let's take just a minute and further analyze this accident.

Begin by stating the problem, in this case: "Richard slipped on water in the basement, fell, and broke his arm."

Next, start asking "Why."

Why? "Because there was water on the floor," the most apparent answer.

Why? "Because the boiler was leaking."

Why? "Because we hired a contractor who presented the lowest bid, a process that took three weeks. When we called to schedule the repair last week, that contractor was too busy to respond. We were waiting to hear back from our purchasing department about how to proceed."

Why? "Because our purchasing procedures state that we accept the lowest bid and go through the procurement department for any repairs over $1,000."

Why? "Because that is what our procurement policy states for any facility maintenance issues."

When supervisors ask "why" enough times, the central problem or problems appear. Requiring that the department accept the lowest bid and the lengthy timeline for repairs are the likely causes of this accident. A change to bidding procedures or improved communication between departments may eliminate accidents of this nature.

Other variables may have influenced the fall, such as failing to post signs or poor lighting. Whoever performs the analysis must be methodical enough to find all contributing factors. In addition to revisiting the procurement code, supervisors could implement or enforce other policies.

Five "whys" is not a magic number. It may take fewer or more than five. But it's a solid investigative tool that can help determine the root cause(s).

Money is a strong motivator. Make claim frequency a part of the managers' bonus criteria. Fewer injuries or accidents would increase a manager's bonus. Hit their wallet and you have their undivided attention.

Let's review how to form and manage the loss prevention committee, an organization's risk management heartbeat.

CHAPTER EIGHT - LOSS PREVENTION COMMITTEES HELP REDUCE ACCIDENTS AND BOOST PROFITS

A loss prevention committee can quickly and dramatically reduce your accidents and improve your loss history. Here are the most important steps in forming an effective loss prevention committee.

Senior Management Creates The Safety Culture

I know many safety professionals. All of them I have spoken with agree – safety starts at the top of the organization. It is management's responsibility to create a safe culture. The front-line employees of an organization cannot push safety uphill.

What is a safety culture? The basis for all the many definitions is this short, sweet, and spot-on principle: Safety comes before profit. Many organizations with strong safety records begin each meeting with a safety report. Senior management sets the tone – safety is a key part of our success. Safety never takes a back seat to profitability. In fact, a safe organization is a key factor in its financial success.

But building a safety culture requires more than adopting a "safety first" principle. In a safe organization, training is ongoing from the first day of hire. Safety equals profitability. This develops "safety first" attitudes in both management and employees. Those attitudes form the basis of a commitment to the organization's health and safety. Managers set the safety culture. Employees embrace safety because they hear about its importance each day.

Senior Management Should Create And Distribute A Loss Prevention Policy Statement

A loss prevention statement, according to the State of Arizona Risk Management Department, is "a written document signed by the director that communicates upper management support and commitment to the agency's loss prevention program."

This should be a straightforward, one-page statement that clearly describes your organization's safety philosophy. It reinforces management's commitment to safety.

Choose Dependable And Well-Respected Employees To Serve On The Committee

Your employees will respect the committee only if they respect its members. Your committee may involve mostly front-line supervisors and managers. However, it is important to include a few front-line employees. These employees know what happens at the worksite or on the shop floor. Choose front-line employees who have the respect of their coworkers but also have the courage to take difficult stands. Membership on the safety committee is also an effective way to groom front-liners to become supervisors.

Determine The Committee's Reach

Will your committee review near misses as well as accidents and injuries? Will its members develop the standards for inspections? Will they perform those inspections? Your committee members must understand where their responsibilities begin and end. They need to know what resources they have to solve problems.

A loss prevention committee that acts randomly will lose respect quickly. One that hands out orders to supervisors or employees will fail. Committee members must work with supervisors to achieve acceptance from supervisors and employees.

Some committees focus solely on safety and near misses. Others have a broader vision and include organizational issues like those listed below.

- Environmental concerns
- Equipment maintenance and reliability
- Quality control

It is critical that no subject is taboo for your committee as long as managers understand the subject and the information is appropriate. For example, you don't want your committee discussing something that may violate one of your employee's medical privacy rights. A senior manager well-versed in human resource management should serve on the committee or at least monitor the agenda.

Determine Committee Authority

Should anything be off-limits to the loss prevention committee? To reduce workforce resistance, be careful not to overdo the committee's authority at first. Senior management must set the limits of authority and ensure committee members operate within that authority.

Issues may arise that are outside the committee's authority. If that happens, the committee chairperson should consult with management to determine how to proceed. This is especially true when human resource issues such as job modification, safety violations, or other performance issues arise.

It is easy to overly control the committee or restrict them to minor issues, according to many safety professionals. A committee in name only is a waste of time. However, you must tread carefully at first to gain acceptance in your organization. Change is rarely easy. It takes time for front-line employees to trust the committee. You also want to ensure your committee doesn't create legal liability with agendas, minutes, and other committee documents. One early misstep can derail your committee.

What Topics Should The Committee Avoid?

Should workers' compensation claims be off-limits to the loss prevention committee? Is your committee empowered to conduct post-accident investigations? Can it direct corrective action? Do committee members have the expertise to suggest engineering modifications? Can they change a corporate policy? Before you begin and as the committee evolves, your organization must discuss these issues.

Understand the importance of protecting medical information. You can disclose medical information only on a "need to know" basis. For example, after an injury, employees may inquire about the medical condition of that employee. Your response should be generic. "S/he is getting the best medical care."

The title "supervisor" or "manager" doesn't automatically entitle that person to medical information. Only if your supervisors need specific information to accommodate a return to work should they discuss medical information and only as it relates to making the temporary or permanent accommodation for modified duty or return to work.

Often senior managers involve themselves in trivia or overreact to minor issues, safety experts report. This kind of reaction speaks loudly to employees and undermines management's credibility. The best committee members know they are facilitators who help supervisors and employees obtain the resources they need to solve their departmental safety problems.

When Will Your Committee Meet?

In smaller organizations, a quarterly meeting may be sufficient. Initially, however, your committee will need to meet more frequently as members develop committee policies and your organization's loss prevention manual. Each meeting should have a formal agenda. A committee secretary should write minutes and action items at each meeting. Beware of writing down items that a savvy trial attorney might later subpoena in a lawsuit. For example, writing down that an accident is "chargeable," or someone is "at fault," can come back to bite you if it ends up as a trial exhibit. Remember, the committee's task is to improve safety, not assign blame.

Your agenda will help to guide each meeting. It also builds a history of the steps your company takes to improve safety. Your committee must identify who will follow up on each item. One of the biggest problems I have seen with safety committees is that they often fail to assign someone to fix problems. They point out, "Oh, this latch is broken" or "Someone fell on that sidewalk where the tree roots raised it." But no one fixes the problem.

Here's what can happen. Your committee addresses a problem and requests a correction in one meeting. An assigned person fixes the problem but fails to document that fix before the next meeting. And no one asks who corrected the problem. In another scenario, your meeting minutes show that someone reported the problem. But, darn, no one fixed it.

Trying to defend that lack of action in a liability claim will fail.

Safety Committees Should Solve Problems, Not Assign Blame

If you launch a safety committee in your organization, you can expect some employee resistance, at first. They may refer to your committee as a "kangaroo court" or spread rumors that "heads will roll." To avoid this as you roll out your committee, publicize the intent of the committee.

Your intent should be clear – not to assign blame, but to determine how to prevent future, similar occurrences. Sure, employees make mistakes. Resolving those issues, however, is a supervisory or a training task for outside the committee. When employees make mistakes, the supervisor is responsible to ensure those mistakes don't happen again. If you run your committee thinking solutions and not blame, employees will soon support the committee and may even offer to get involved.

Here is an example of how a committee I formed worked. One of our employees had an incident that resulted in a trailer coming loose from the truck, damaging the trailer. The employee had used the wrong size ball for the hitch on the trailer. His supervisor presented the claim to the risk management department. We scheduled the employee and his supervisor to attend the next committee meeting to explain what happened.

The employee nervously appeared with his boss straight from the field in his work pants and work boots. He explained that he didn't realize that balls and hitches came in assorted sizes. He assumed they were one-size-fits-all.

We wanted to prevent that type of accident. We asked him if he would consider presenting "tailgate training." In it, he would teach his coworkers how to recognize and choose the right size ball for the hitch. He readily agreed to do so, and with a little help from his supervisor, completed the training. His entire work unit benefited from the short training session. He learned two lessons, how to choose the right ball for the hitch and how to present what he'd learned. And he didn't feel punished.

When employees understand that they are accountable for their actions, but the repercussions from the committee are relatively positive, they begin to trust the process and support your committee.

Of course, some accidents require disciplinary action. You should avoid discussing some incidents headed for litigation. However, most incidents your company experiences will be perfectly good items for your committee.

The Benefits Of A Safety Committee

When companies experience fewer incidents due to a well-run loss prevention committee, support for the committee will grow. It won't take long to see results. Many businesses that implement a loss prevention committee see impressive reductions in injuries and other mishaps almost immediately. Morale also improves because employees begin to believe that the organization cares about their well-being.

Rather than rely on employee chatter about how your committee functions, each year ask your members to complete a committee self-evaluation. Ask questions such as these.

- Agendas accurately reflect what we discuss
- All committee members feel free to respectfully voice their opinions
- All committee members have a positive attitude toward the meetings
- Committee members receive the training they need to function effectively on the committee
- Follow-through by the supervisors and managers is adequate
- Management at all levels support the committee
- Minutes are accurate and timely

A well-functioning safety committee is a key factor in controlling your TCOR.

Now let's review the importance of prompt injury reporting.

CHAPTER NINE - PROMPT INJURY REPORTING ESSENTIAL IN MANAGING CLAIM COSTS

Adjusters have a tough time investigating accident claims that have a long "lag time." This is the time between the date the incident occurs and the date you report that claim to your workers' compensation insurer. The more quickly you report workplace incidents to your insurance carrier, the less your injuries will cost to settle. Smaller claims costs result in a lower emod and reduced premiums. Short lag time can also prevent an injury from becoming a lengthy, problematic injury or a permanent disability.

Why Report Injuries Promptly?

Many insurance industry studies validate that the greater the lag time, the more the claim costs to settle. One study conducted by the NCCI reported that a claim with a lag time of over four weeks cost almost 32 percent more than similar injuries promptly reported.

Employers sometimes refuse to report an injury to their insurer when they question the incident's validity. Report suspicious injuries like any other injury. Even if you are sure the injury did not occur as reported, always report it promptly. However, be sure you tell your adjuster your suspicions. It may be better to avoid documenting doubts in writing, so call the adjuster instead.

Here are a few of the many reasons to report injuries promptly.

- Immediate intervention by the adjuster to manage the medical treatment reduces costs. When adjusters move in quickly to manage care with more appropriate providers, costs will drop.

- On suspect claims, investigate the facts promptly before memories fade or internal alliances shift. Workers who allege an injury may pressure other employees to side with them, even when a coworker knows the injury did not occur as reported.

- Many states impose penalties for late reporting. Your state may fine the insurer for failure to issue wage benefits in a timely manner.

- Many states require insurance companies to accept or reject claims within a certain number of days. If you file a late report, your adjuster may deny the claim before completing the investigation to comply with state statutes. This rejection can cause your employee to hire an attorney.

- Workers who receive prompt attention after an injury are less likely to hire attorneys. Attorney involvement increases costs.

The longer the reporting delay, the more an injury will cost and the more likely your employee will lose time from work. Even one day of employee lost time can impact your emod.

Here are some ways to help you reduce reporting time and lower claims costs.

Develop And Formalize Injury Reporting Protocol

Your employees must understand that they should report all incidents immediately, even if they are not sure they are injured.

A hit-and-run driver struck one of our employees in his brand-new work van he'd customized himself. He was proud of his work, so naturally, he was furious. Our manager went to the scene and waited with him for the highway patrol to arrive. Our employee wanted to go to the emergency room to "sue the heck out of that guy when they catch him." He wasn't hurt; he was angry. I asked if he was in pain anywhere. He wasn't. I then said, "He probably won't have any assets anyway. Why don't you see how you feel tomorrow?"

He agreed and the next day, felt fine. He did not need medical treatment, he needed to have someone acknowledge his anger.

You can't interfere with an employee's decision to treat. I'm not suggesting that. You can, however, debrief an employee post-injury to help determine if s/he needs immediate treatment at an emergency room. If not, the employee may be able to wait a day and see an occupational doctor if needed.

Your supervisors and managers should know how to report the injury to the insurance carrier as quickly as possible. I've repeatedly seen delays in reporting because supervisors "couldn't find the form." Most internal protocols require employees to report injuries to their supervisor the same day they occur and before shift end. If the employee seeks medical treatment, that report should go to the carrier immediately and in no case more than 24 hours after the in-house first notice.

First, the insurer processes the claim. Then, and only then, the adjuster can begin to manage medical care where allowed. Even a promptly reported injury may take up to 48 hours for the adjuster to call your employee and begin managing care. A lot of medical care can occur in 48 hours.

Why Managing Medical Care Is Critical

Forty states give insurers and their adjusters the statutory right to manage the medical portion of a claim. Ten states let the injured employees manage their medical treatment. When employees or attorneys manage care, results are "Not good," according to James Moore, a workers' compensation consultant and founder of J&L Risk Management Consultants in Raleigh, North Carolina.

Adjusters know the best physicians for the problem, not the employee or local attorneys. In addition, each day that your employee or your employee's attorney manages the medical part of the claim, costs increase, in most cases.

The right to manage care for workers' compensation insurers is wide open for legislative improvement, according to Moore. Encourage your chamber of commerce to lobby for changes if you're in a state that disallows adjuster medical management.

Develop Internal Protocols To Improve Injury Reporting

Each state has different injury reporting requirements. You should be familiar with those requirements. However, procedures that your state suggests may be far from best management practices. Develop your own protocols and then train to those protocols. This is the best way to ensure timely reporting.

Many supervisors do not realize how crucial reporting promptly is to claim value. Make sure your entire staff knows about the cost increases that occur when companies fail to promptly report injuries. Use employee orientation, written reminders, and safety training to remind employees about their role in prompt reporting. Hold supervisors and employees accountable for late reports. Then they will be more likely to submit appropriate paperwork immediately. Employees must understand that failure to report injuries timely may risk their benefits and could result in disciplinary action. If reminded, they will understand the importance of prompt reporting.

Consider A 1-800 Injury Reporting Line

Many organizations now turn to nurse call centers to report all injuries. These call centers specialize in workers' compensation injury management from the first call through ongoing medical management, if needed. They are staffed 24/7/365 with occupational nurses who help reduce unnecessary medical treatment, direct medical care, and avoid emergency room visits whenever possible.

The goal is to determine the need for on-site first aid treatment or medical treatment. With the help of an industrial nurse on the phone, the employee can self-apply first aid like heat or ice. The nurse will refer the injured employee to an appropriate occupational medical doctor or urgent care if needed. Medical providers help preselect medical offices geographically. These medical providers are well-versed in industrial medicine and return-to-work protocols. Most employees appreciate the nurse triage process.

Studies show nurse first-call initiatives reduce costs and improve return-to-work outcomes. One 2020 study completed by first-call provider Company Nurse with its client Everest Insurance showed outstanding results. Giving the injured worker initial access to licensed nurses provided Everest Insurance with these savings.

- A 55 percent reduction in the average total claims costs
- A 41 percent reduction in lag time
- A 25 percent reduction in average claim duration
- A 56 percent reduction in litigation rates

First-call nurse triage can help avoid doctor and emergency room visits and get claims started on the right foot.

While employers with more than 100 employees usually implement nursing triage, smaller employers can benefit, as well. According to Debra Spamer, Vice President of Business Development at Company Nurse, "As one small employer told me, it only takes one claim going off the rails to sink our business."

Nurse triage is another program designed to help reduce workers' compensation claims costs.

Provide Incentives For Prompt Reporting And Reaching Safety Goals

Prompt injury reporting should be part of your supervisors' annual goals. Their bonuses should reflect, in part, how quickly employees report their injuries. Encourage supervisors to report at least quarterly the methods they use to promote safety and encourage timely reporting. Unless employees at all levels feel accountable for safety, they will often put other business goals ahead of working safely.

No injury or accident should go uninvestigated. Someone in the organization should be accountable when something goes wrong, especially when poor supervision or training results in an injury. Only if the appropriate person acts in accordance with the company's reporting procedures will employees take safety seriously.

Temporarily Redeploy Personnel

If your organization is experiencing problems with prompt reporting, redeploy personnel to help. A manager who can oversee the process and work out the kinks can target reporting processes for improvement. If needed, hire a consultant or ask your insurance broker or carrier if they can assist.

Many studies show the cost increases on late-reported claims, so prompt reporting should be a company-wide priority. Prompt reporting will reduce your emod and lower your total cost of risk.

Next, let's discuss how to best build relationships with your carrier's adjusting team.

CHAPTER TEN - TO REDUCE COSTS, DEVELOP RELATIONSHIPS WITH YOUR ADJUSTERS

The most critical element in managing a work-related injury is effective communication. This means you must communicate effectively with your adjuster if an employee sustains an injury. Your adjuster, the insurer's claims person, is critical to managing your employee's injury and closing the claim.

Even before your first injury occurs, build a solid rapport with your adjusters. If your facility is close to their office, visit them. You also could invite them to visit you. Your adjusters will get to know your managers and supervisors and come to understand how your business works. They'll learn who to call for an incident investigation and to help return employees to work after an injury. They'll be better able to evaluate an accident and whether your employee's injury is consistent with the operations your company typically performs.

An employee injury can take on a life of its own when you cannot get the employee well and back to work. A number of reasons can lead to this frustrating situation. Within the first few weeks or months of hiring, an employee sometimes "sets up" your company for an injury. Other times, though, a lack of communication plus inadequate claims management is squarely to blame for an employee's continuing disability.

Adjusters today often don't receive the many months of training that was typical in the past. They may earn a degree and find themselves behind an adjuster's desk without all the knowledge they need. The insurance industry, like many other industries, is experiencing a wave of brain drain as experienced employees retire. With experienced adjusters leaving, promotions may occur long before that person is ready.

Forming a partnership with your adjuster before injuries happen means stronger claims management. A strong relationship will also help ensure that your employees receive the superior medical treatment they deserve.

Steps To Take Before You Buy Coverage

Before you buy coverage with a workers' compensation insurance company, try to establish which adjusters will work on your account. Small employers won't be able to have much influence in this area. However, as your business grows and your premiums increase, you can have more input into these decisions.

You need highly experienced adjusters assigned to your company. If you're a larger account, ask to review the resumes of the adjusters who will handle your claims. You may get pushback, but you want to be sure that your adjusters are qualified. If not, the lack of experience will ultimately cost you in higher claim payouts, which means higher premiums.

You want experienced adjusters. They usually achieve the best results. Experienced adjusters know almost intuitively which employees are "working the system" and which are trying to get well and return to work. They know the best medical providers for the type of injury.

Not All Medical Treatment Is Equal

The American Bar Association cited a National Academy of Medicine report that stated, "Racial and ethnic minorities receive lower-quality medical care than White people – even when insurance status, income, age, and severity of injury are comparable." Many adjusters understand that differences in gender, race, and socio-economic status can greatly impact the quality of medical treatment your employee will receive. An adjuster sensitive to this reality will advocate for your employees.

You also want adjusters to carry reasonable caseloads. The number of claims, or the caseload, assigned to an adjuster often outnumbers industry standards. Too large caseloads will cause your organization's claims handling to suffer.

Average caseloads vary by injury severity and jurisdiction. However, make sure the adjusters assigned to your company manage fewer than about 125 open lost-time claims. Otherwise, results will suffer, delaying your employees' return to work and increasing claim payouts.

Try To Place All Your Business Insurance With One Insurer

Especially for smaller companies, I strongly recommend you place all your coverage with one insurance company if you can. You can choose to bundle, such as a businessowners policy with workers' compensation coverage. Or you could place standalone coverages with the same carrier.

Before I married into my husband's "plumbing dynasty," I handled his insurance. Because we were so small at the time, few insurers were willing to write our coverage. We placed the general and auto liability with one carrier and bought a standalone workers' compensation policy from a different carrier that specialized in workers' compensation. Our second year into the policy period, one of our plumbers suffered a hernia trying to lift a half-emptied water heater, obviously a safety violation. After more than 30 years in business, it was the first claim of any kind for this business. The carrier paid about $12,000 on the claim. When renewal time rolled around, the insurer refused to renew our coverage.

I spoke to two of their marketing people, who were dismissive. Their scoffing response to my non-renewal inquiry was to ask, "So how much did we pay on that claim?" I told them the number.

"But aren't you in the business of paying claims?" I asked. They just looked at each other.

We changed carriers and agents at that time, choosing an agent with a greater choice of insurers. We moved to a carrier that now writes most of our coverages, business auto, general liability, the umbrella, commercial property, and of course, our workers' compensation coverage.

Why is this important? A carrier that insures only your workers' compensation coverage has no other income to balance any losses. If you have an injury claim, you're much likelier to get non-renewed. Non-renewal can leave you in a bind because other carriers will take a closer look at your account if they even agree to consider covering you. If you lose your coverage, you may end up in an assigned risk plan.

Assigned risk plans are safety nets for employers unable to buy coverage in the standard insurance market. Assigned risk plan rates are generally higher. Trust me, you do not want to end up there.

Workers' compensation coverage is necessary for business solvency. Monopolistic states require you to purchase their option – state-run coverage. All other states have an assigned risk plan. If you are currently in an assigned risk plan, work with an agent or consultant who can help you return to the standard insurance market. This happens only by improving your safety practices and reducing your injuries.

If your payroll provider offers workers' compensation coverage, you may choose that coverage. The upside is that your payroll seamlessly corresponds to your actual payroll. This can help you avoid audit charges at year-end if you've underreported payroll. However, be extremely cautious. Some of the payroll plans are self-insured groups or may offer you a sweet initial rate followed by "rate creep" at renewal, according to one risk management consultant.

Before you decide to go with the carrier your payroll provider offers, talk to your agent or broker.

My advice – work with an agent or broker who has a number of carriers that specialize in your type of organization. Bundle your coverage with one insurer whenever possible. Doing this creates fewer contacts and makes renewals easier to track. Placing all your insurance policies with one insurer also helps if you need advice or loss prevention services.

You Catch More Flies With Honey

When claims go badly, adjusters often hear a great many complaints from managers or business owners. Some of this is just frustration and venting. But remember, adjusters receive plenty of on-the-job medical and other training. They pride themselves on their professionalism. The adjuster's job is to correctly manage your employee's medical treatment. It is not the adjuster's fault when an employee fails to heal or perhaps malingers. You don't want to be the client who constantly loses your temper or criticizes your adjusters. If you behave this way, your adjusters may avoid calling you. If problems arise, you may find yourself left out of some important loops.

If you experience a problem with a claim, talk with your adjuster before you call his or her supervisor. Give the adjuster a chance to clarify the situation. You may learn exactly why your employee is not recovering and what the adjuster is doing to return that employee to work or to close the claim.

Be nice. Be known as that person who is calm and acts, not reacts, to updates and claim problems.

What Happens When An Employee Doesn't Recover?

The adjuster's goal in every workplace injury is to return the injured employee to maximum medical improvement (MMI) through appropriate medical treatment. MMI occurs when the employee's medical condition is "as good as it's going to get," in layperson's terms. The employee may have fully recovered or may need future treatment. However, their medical condition will not improve. It is the goal of the adjuster, with appropriate medical treatment, to get the employee to MMI.

When an employee is not recovering according to normal disability guidelines, the adjuster may tell you, "S/he is not MMI." Ask the adjuster this critical question: "What is your plan of action to resolve this injury?" The adjuster should provide you with a detailed recovery plan that will return the employee to work, resolve the injury, or move the employee to the next level of medical treatment. That next level may be a specialist or a surgical intervention. Or it may be appropriate to schedule a setting in front of an administrative law judge to move the claim along.

Here is a typical action plan for an employee with a shoulder injury who is still in pain despite six weeks of physical therapy. The doctor now recommends shoulder surgery.

- Determine if an arthroscopic procedure can restore the shoulder. An arthroscope is a tool that uses fiber optics to repair a joint. Arthroscopic repair reduces costs, employee impairment, and lost workdays.
- If the employee requires surgery, schedule that surgery.
- Establish which provider will provide physical therapy

post-injury.

- Talk with the supervisor to determine how to return the employee to work within his or her restrictions.
- Assign a nurse case manager if healing does not occur within normal disability timelines.
- Review reserves to ensure reserve adequacy.

Without a plan of action, claims tend to drift. Communication between the employee, the adjuster, and the employer begins to break down.

Only when a claim has a solid action plan do more serious injuries resolve in reasonable time frames.

Develop Reasonable Performance Standards With Your Insurance Carrier

From the outset of your relationship with your insurance carrier, you should agree on reasonable performance standards. Here are a few of the most frequent standards insisted on by larger clients who carry significant deductibles on their insurance. However, these standards should be part of any insurer's workers' compensation claims performance guidelines.

- Three-point contact within twenty-four hours of an injury.
  o Three-point contact means the adjuster talks to the injured worker, the supervisor or human resources liaison, and the treating physician or his or her office staff. This contact is crucial, even if your adjuster only reviews the medical report. Three-point contact helps reduce the likelihood that an injured employee will hire an attorney. It ensures the physician immediately furnishes appropriate medical reports to determine the extent of the injury.
- Status reports at appropriate intervals.
  o Many larger employers meet quarterly with their adjusting team, either virtually or in person. In this meeting, discuss all

open claims to learn each injured employee's status and what the adjuster's action plan is for file resolution. Review and resolve any return-to-work issues you may experience as employees transition back to work.

- Supervisors review the file and provide oversight frequently throughout the life of a claim.

o Many adjusters are excellent injury managers. But too often inexperienced adjusters allow employees to manage their own treatment. They may also rely too heavily on nurse case management, which can increase claims costs needlessly. Medical oversight helps keep employees from malingering or directing their own medical treatment.

- Appropriate subrogation when other parties caused your employee's injury.

Even smaller insureds should insist on the above performance standards. Once you have agreed on performance standards, meet with your adjuster at least quarterly. Online meetings work well. Review all open claims to discuss the injury and review reserves.

No matter how upset you get with your carrier or adjuster, remember that you are not adversaries. You are better off if you conduct your relationship as a partnership. This means more than just building a relationship with your adjusters. You must first agree with your carrier on sound claims service protocols.

These steps will function properly only if you practice frequent and open communication and a culture of teamwork between your managers and your carrier's adjusters.

Communication Is Key To Successful Claims Closure

After any industrial injury, your best tools for limiting the costs associated with an injury are effective communication and highly experienced adjusters. When you forge a strong relationship with your adjusters, you reduce the possibility that one injury becomes a major cost driver in your workers' compensation program.

Next, let's discuss the importance of adding the services of a nurse case manager to several types of injuries.

CHAPTER ELEVEN - NURSE CASE MANAGEMENT CAN REDUCE COSTS AND IMPROVE MEDICAL OUTCOMES

Every business owner wants to send his or her employees home safely each day. The reality is, though, that employees do get injured. And when they do, a nurse case manager can help keep your employee's injury moving toward recovery.

While your insurance carrier handles the hiring and management of nurse case managers (NCMs), sometimes adjusters ignore these highly effective practitioners. You can help by suggesting the careful use of these experts in the following circumstances.

- When your employee alleges an unwitnessed or unsubstantiated injury
- When your employee is seriously or catastrophically injured, such as a traumatic brain or back injury
- When your employee, despite treatment, fails to recover
- When English is your employee's second language

What Is A Nurse Case Manager?

He or she is a highly skilled nurse who specializes in managing workers' compensation injuries. NCMs know the best industrial physicians, can talk medical terms to your employee's providers, and act as a conduit for accurate information about your employees' job functions. Often times the information between your employee and his or her physician is one-sided. Your employee may not always accurately portray the work environment to avoid returning to work. In some cases, s/he may be malingering. A NCM is an effective approach to ensure that communication between the adjuster, the employee, and the physician accurately reflects the circumstances.

Hiring nurse case management may seem like an added cost. After all, the insurer bills the cost back to your employee's claim. One Liberty Mutual Insurance Company study, however, showed an astounding eight-to-one return on investment.

NCMs do more than reduce claim costs by managing the medical portion of a claim. They also help return injured employees to work more quickly by encouraging them to follow doctor's orders. NCMs usually know the best doctors for the injury type. They can attend medical appointments to improve communication between patient and doctor. Adjusters often talk directly to employees after seeing a doctor. However, not all employees leave doctor appointments understanding what the doctor said. This is one area where nurse case management can be vital.

No manager wants to see one of his or her employees injured, especially catastrophically. However, if a severe injury like a spinal cord or brain injury does occur, your carrier should immediately assign a NCM to oversee the medical care. In catastrophic injuries, quick decisions and family support are vital to the employee's recovery and adjustment post treatment. The nurse will go to the hospital and talk with doctors and the family. The NCM will greatly improve communication with family members and doctors. The NCM is also a tremendous help to the family caregiver in catastrophic injuries. A case manager is not a luxury in these cases, but a necessary provider who will ensure your employee gets the best medical care available while ultimately reducing costs.

Nurse case managers receive highly specialized training in occupational injury management. They help ensure your employee receives appropriate medical treatment.

What About Injuries That Just Don't Heal?

Many organizations face some situations that baffle both the company and its adjusters – injured employees who do not get well. Often, no one can point to any single issue that prevents healing. Delayed healing sometimes continues because the adjuster has run out of ideas to manage the injury. Delays in recovery can also occur because chronic conditions such as diabetes hinder healing. This is when hiring a NCM will pay big dividends.

The nurse becomes your employee's advocate, ensuring the following.

- The medical provider makes the best medical decisions for the patient
- Everyone involved in the injury – the employer, the family, and the patient – understands the treatment plan

In non-catastrophic injuries, the NCM normally meets with your employee's treating physician at the employee's appointment. The NCM will talk to the doctor and help to make sure the employee and the adjuster understand the current medical status. Employees sometimes tell doctors only one side of the story – theirs – especially when describing their job duties.

The nurse reviews the essential job functions to help the doctor implement a speedy return to work. Just like in any profession, you will find exceedingly talented physicians and those who are average or even below average. They all differ in the quality of treatment they render. Additionally, a perfectly competent surgeon can have a bad outcome.

However, NCMs know which surgeons consistently outperform others and which hospitals have lower complication rates like secondary infections. They also help employees understand "medical-ese," what their physicians are telling them.

Good NCMs will help evaluate an employee's need for other medical interventions. They may suggest the adjuster order an independent medical examination (IME) by a specialized or non-treating physician. In an IME, the doctor reviews all medical records and examines the patient to determine the employee's physical complaints. The doctor has no treatment relationship with the injured employee. He or she is solely there to determine whether former medical treatment is appropriate, how to proceed medically, or in the early claim stage, help determine if the injury arose from employment.

After each visit, the NCM updates the adjuster about the employee's medical condition. This allows the adjuster to revisit reserve adequacy. It helps the adjuster determine if the employee can safely return to temporary modified duty if it's available.

Nurses Help Eliminate Language Barriers

When an employee speaks English as a second language, a visit to the doctor can be bewildering. Add difficult medical terms and your baffled injured employee may become depressed or feel humiliated. An employee with limited language skills may not ask questions. Instead, they may politely listen to the doctor, who walks out of the room believing the employee understood the doctor's words or directions. A worker may refuse to cooperate with treating physicians. However, this could be more from confusion than stubbornness.

Some case managers speak other languages, especially in urban areas and along border towns like Nogales or El Paso. If a worker has no immigration documentation, essential information such as date of birth may be inaccurate. This often contributes to an incomplete medical background that can hamper diagnosis and delay healing.

Employees who speak English as a second language may hire attorneys. This will increase claims costs. You might be able to prevent this by using a NCM early in the process who is fluent in the injured worker's native language. If an injured employee lacks immigration documents, a NCM can help in several ways, including those listed below.

- Communicate with family members who speak no English but are involved in patient care
- Help to locate injured employees who move multiple times
- Reassure the employee who may have a basic mistrust of the system
- Work through issues like substandard living conditions

When workers speak limited English, a bilingual nurse provides a strong return on investment.

When used thoughtfully, a good NCM will reduce claim costs and lost-time workdays. An experienced adjuster should be able to manage most injuries. However, in a severe injury or when recovery fails to match disability recovery guidelines, a NCM can help close the claim.

Now, let's review the basics of setting up a solid Stay-at-Work/Return-to-Work (SAW/RTW) program to bring employees back to work quickly post-injury.

CHAPTER TWELVE - STAY-AT-WORK/ RETURN-TO-WORK PROGRAMS MAY PROVIDE YOUR BIGGEST SAVINGS

One of the most effective ways you can prevent needless work loss and disability is by building a strong stay-at-work/return-to-work program. This program enables you to keep good employees and reduce your workers' compensation premiums.

Reducing Collateral Damage In Injury Claims

Any workplace injury is disturbing to your employees. But the consequences from an injury don't stop with payouts on the claim and disruption to the employee's lifestyle. Workplace injuries also

- reduce productivity when injured workers lose time from work while they heal,
- lower morale when other workers feel that they bear an unequal work burden or that managers fumbled on safety, and

- reduce profitability as you scramble to pay replacement labor or overtime.

A well-planned SAW/RTW program will help.

What Is Saw/Rtw?

SAW/RTW is the process that returns injured employees to work as quickly as possible after a workplace accident. Studies have repeatedly shown that the longer an injured employee is away from work, the greater his or her chances of never returning to employment. Studies also confirm that a SAW/RTW program minimizes the impact of workplace injuries for both employee and employer, benefitting all.

The goal of the SAW/RTW process is to step-by-step advance an injured employee from absence, through limited work status, to full working capability. SAW/RTW is not a permanent accommodation of a disability. However, employers may face such a decision when an employee suffers a permanent, work-related impairment. That discussion is outside the scope of this book. I suggest if you face this issue, you hire a consultant or talk with an employment attorney rather than make decisions that can backfire.

SAW/RTW is the program that helps an employee, once injured, return to some form of meaningful work as quickly as possible post-injury.

Many doubts surround return to work. Here are a few reasons managers and physicians may feel reluctant to return an injured employee to work.

- What if the employee reinjures him or herself?
- Why should my department pay an employee to be unproductive?
- Will the supervisor devote the time needed to monitor an injured employee?

- As a physician, can I trust that your supervisors will honor the limitations of my return-to-work directive?

A well-managed SAW/RTW program addresses these issues. If properly developed and managed, the risks of a return to work are small and the rewards are tremendous. Here are just a few of the many benefits of a SAW/RTW program.

- A well-crafted program helps your organization avoid ADA litigation. After the ADA's amendment in 2008, no longer could employees tell their injured workers, "You cannot return to work until you can perform 100 percent of your job."

- Employees feel supported and appreciated. This includes both those with injuries and those impacted by their coworkers' extended absences.

- Employees who otherwise might never return to work come back to productive employment.

- Rather than staying at home after an injury, your SAW/RTW program keeps injured employees at work, helping reduce depression, which often delays healing.

- SAW/RTW provides a clear structure to better manage injuries.

- SAW/RTW saves you money because the insurance carrier pays less in temporary total disability. This reduction translates to a lower premium.

- When employees know they will return to work post-injury, your SAW/RTW philosophy discourages malingering and can reduce or even prevent the filing of fraudulent claims.

Elements Of The Saw/Rtw Program

Here are some of the key steps in a SAW/RTW program.

- Create accurate job descriptions – An accurate and thorough job description sets expectations for the employee. It also allows for a solid pre-employment physical to determine if the employee can perform the essential functions of that position. Your job description should clearly outline the physical demands of the position. When an employee loses time from work, be sure to furnish that job description to the treating physician. This can help develop effective SAW/RTW accommodations.

- Pre-establish alternate-duty positions – If you wait until an injury sidelines an employee, it may take you a week or more to find alternative work. This increases costs and may mean the employee feels neglected. By developing alternate duty positions before an injury occurs, you can return an employee the day of or the day after the treating physician clears the employee for modified work. Always send the treating physician a copy of the employee's alternate position. This makes doctors feel more comfortable releasing their patients back to temporary modified duty.

- Prepare a written temporary modified-duty offer – This offer should list the modified duties the employee will perform. Always use the word "temporary." This ensures employees do not think you're creating permanent positions for them in case they do not recover enough to resume their former positions. Both employer and employee should sign this document. It can be critical in terminating disability benefits if the employee refuses the temporary position or abandons the position. If the employee refuses to sign the offer, then document the refusal and forward your internal documentation immediately to your adjuster.

- Develop a communication process – All involved should understand how information flows. For example, does the injured employee report to his or her former supervisor, to a human resource professional, or to his or her temporary supervisor? Clear communication that is well documented is critical to the success of your SAW/RTW program.

It's essential supervisors do not let returning employees perform tasks that conflict with the physical limitations imposed by the doctor. This is a setup for another injury claim.

Some Final Facts About The Saw/Rtw Approach

Establish a workplace committee of a human resource professional and several managers to develop your program. Use an outside consultant or see if your agent or insurer can assist. Implementing a solid SAW/RTW program

- helps you retain high-quality employees who might otherwise never return to work,
- reduces lost-work days, and
- reduces claims costs.

When you hire, set this expectation – our organization believes in return-to-work. You can state this in supervisory discussions with new employees, in an employee handbook, and in training sessions. Ensure employees understand that you'll do everything in your power to accommodate disabilities. Your goal is to return employees to some type of productivity.

Here are a few temporary modified duty suggestions for returning employees.

- Help with clerical functions.
- Help organize storage and other neglected areas.
- Send your employee to a local non-profit to help, wearing your company's gear.
- Watch safety or attend other training.

These activities will help reduce workers' compensation payouts and help to protect your emod.

Most insurers can assist you in developing an effective SAW/RTW program. For larger organizations, bringing in a consultant will create a swift return on investment.

Next, let's discuss the importance of understanding your experience modification factor, one of the most important criteria in developing your premium.

CHAPTER THIRTEEN - UNDERSTANDING YOUR EXPERIENCE MODIFICATION FACTOR

Did you ever wonder how an insurance carrier calculates your insurance premium? Your experience modification factor emod is a critical element to estimating your rate – the amount your insurer charges according to your class codes and payroll – and your premium. Understanding your emod factor is critical in controlling your premiums.

Your emod is one of the most important metrics used by your insurance carrier to determine your premium. Your emod is based on your organization's safety record. Here are the three basic functions of your emod, according to Bill Wilson, an expert in insurance and author of *When Words Collide: Resolving Insurance Coverage and Claims Disputes*.

1. Your emod compares your organization's actual loss experience to other average risks of the same type. For example, if you're a general contractor, it will compare you against other general contractors.

2. Your emod helps your insurance carrier predict your fu-

ture loss experience.

3. Your emod incentivizes your organization to implement loss prevention techniques that will help reduce or eliminate losses.

Your business starts with a 1.00 emod. After three complete years of claims experience, the rating bureau will either increase or decrease your emod based on your organization's loss history. Once your organization acquires an emod, the rating agency will notify you.

If your emod is below 1.00, you'll receive a credit on your premium. Consider that credit a safety reward. If your emod is over 1.00, the carrier will surcharge your premium. If your premium is $10,000 before applying the emod and your emod is 1.07, your premium will be $10,700. If your emod is .97, your premium would be $9,700.

In calculating your emod, the rating agency weighs claims frequency as more important than claims severity. Reducing small but frequent losses is important in managing your emod.

Your Emod Is Critical To Managing Your Insurance Premiums

Many experts consider your emod to be a numeric symbol of your safety record and claims history as it compares to other businesses in your class.

Many risk management experts frequently find miscalculated emods. This can cost you an additional premium and may even cause you to lose contracts. According to Ed Priz, author of *Workers' Compensation: A Field Guide for Employers,* miscalculated emods are one of the most common reasons for premium overcharges.

The emod is a factor that adjusts your workers' compensation premium based on your losses for the last three years, not including the most recent policy year. Here's an example.

An emod for a policy period that begins on January 1, 2021, includes claims paid for the policy periods shown below.

- January 1, 2017
- January 1, 2018
- January 1, 2019

The actual emod calculation is more complex than this because it compares your losses with expected losses for a similar business in your industry. However, for our purpose, you should understand that the more frequent your losses and their cost to your insurer, the higher your emod, and the higher your premium.

Your Workers' Compensation Policy Is Not Like Your Commercial Property Policy

With your property policy, you know how much premium you will pay from year to year. Your premium generally remains relatively predictable, even if you have a loss. However, with workers' compensation coverage, the opposite is true. You pay an estimated annual premium based on your estimated payroll and your emod when an underwriter accepts your application.

Your insurer will audit you at the end of each policy period to determine if you submitted an accurate payroll amount and obtained valid certificates of insurance from any subcontractors. In addition, your insurer will apply your emod to your premium. The carrier then adjusts your current year's premium. Even if your policy cancels or non-renews and you move to another carrier, your former carrier will still audit you and you still may owe premium.

What you should focus on is that buying workers' compensation insurance is not like buying your commercial property policy where you know your annual premium before you buy. Workers' compensation estimates your premium based on what the insurer expects to pay for your claims in that policy period. You pay your annual premium based on that and on your payroll estimates.

At the end of each policy period, the insurer reviews what they paid for your losses during that period. Then you pay for your losses over three years for the claims your employees actually experienced. Your workers' compensation policy acts more like a financing tool with your loss costs financed over three years.

This is what makes avoiding losses so important in controlling your workers' compensation premium. In some cases, an emod greater than 1.0 will restrict a contractor's ability to bid on key contracts. This can be a death knoll in the construction industry. Managing the organization's emod is critically important to all business owners, but especially to contractors.

Companies that develop an emod are "experienced rated." Generally, once a company generates more than $3,500 per year in workers' compensation premium, that company acquires an emod. Rating bureaus like the NCCI usually calculate emods. One problem can occur because the carrier has not zeroed out reserves on resolved injuries. Reserves are money set aside to pay a specific claim. Another problem that often arises is that reserves may be set too high. Your agent should review your reserves with you for accuracy and discuss questionable reserves with the insurer's claims staff.

Your emod can cause headaches, for certain. However, an agent well versed in servicing workers' compensation policies should help ensure that your carrier has correctly calculated your emod. As we all know with mathematical errors, they rarely occur in our favor.

Some Key Tips To Follow Prior To Policy Expiration

One highly experienced insurance broker recommends the following.

- Six months before your policy renews, ask your agent to review your claims loss history, called your loss run, with you. If there are errors, ask your agent to have the carrier correct them. Errors could include miscoded payments, claims that remain open in error, or missed or delayed efforts to recover losses from at-fault parties.

- Three months before your policy expires, ask your agent to obtain and review your unit statistical card. In most states, this data provides your rating bureau with the payroll and loss information used to develop your emod.

- At about three months prior to renewal, obtain a copy of your auditor's payroll worksheets and check that all class codes are correct.

- A few weeks after your policy expires, you should receive a letter from your auditor asking for annual payroll data as well as all certificates of insurance for any subcontractors who performed work for you. If you don't receive it, ask for it. It's critical that you respond to the auditor. We'll explain why in Chapter 14.

- Immediately start to gather payroll data needed for the audit. If you don't respond timely, a monetary penalty applies in some states.

Reducing Your Emod Begins With Your Safety Program

As you can see, your emod is critical to managing your workers' compensation premiums. Controlling your emod begins with a safer workplace.

This is a very brief overview of the emod process, a complicated calculation. Your workers' compensation agent should be able to answer any questions about your emod. Now let's talk about managing your workers' compensation premium audit.

CHAPTER FOURTEEN - SURVIVING THE WORKERS' COMPENSATION PREMIUM AUDIT

Workers' compensation is not traditional insurance. As discussed in the previous chapter, your emod is a way to finance your losses over a three-year period. You pay a premium that estimates the cost of your employees' injuries. Your policy covers your losses as needed, but you pay for those losses for the next three years based on your emod.

The workers' compensation audit is standard on all workers' compensation policies. However, you must proactively manage the audit process. You'll face premium audit charges if you under-report payroll or fail to obtain valid certificates of insurance from subcontractors. You'll also face additional premium if the insurer finds you incorrectly classified your employees or paid more in payroll than you estimated at the policy start.

Additional Premium Risks

You risk a large additional premium if an audit uncovers any of the following errors.

- Underreporting payroll. At policy inception or renewal, you estimate your annual payroll costs. Any mistakes in this estimate, if not adjusted quarterly, will cost you at audit. Stories abound of business owners facing thousands of dollars in audit premium.

- Misclassifying employees. Especially in construction classes of business, misclassifying employees may save you money in the short term, but it will really cost you at audit. While you may consider a worker an outside salesperson, your insurer may find that salesperson occasionally works on site. This can change the employee's classification to a different job classification with a higher rate. This hurts at audit.

- Failing to maintain accurate payroll records. You may consider someone who works for you as a 1099 subcontractor. Insurers, and especially administrative law judges who rule on workers' compensation cases, often disagree. Just because you obtain a W9 and believe the worker is a 1099 worker doesn't make it so. If you disregard the Internal Revenue Service definition of an independent contractor, your insurer will hammer you with an additional premium. You may also face sanctions from your state for violating its workers' compensation rules. Track overtime and tips paid to employees separately to avoid premium increases at audit. Insurers do not count overtime and tips as payroll, only the base salary rate. State rules do include bonuses in total payroll in most states.

- Failing to properly vet subcontractors. If you work in the trades, your subcontractors should be licensed contractors. You must have a properly completed certificate of insurance that matches the dates the subcontractors work on the project. Your auditor usually will ask for project or payment dates. If you provide an expired certificate of insurance, your insurer will charge you additional premium for that work.

Some insurers will not surcharge you if you hire sole proprietors without workers' compensation insurance. They'll furnish you with a form for the sole proprietor to sign. You'll have to ask for it; they won't offer it. Some insist you resend the form annually to a subcontractor you use routinely.

To survive your audit, you'll need the following at a minimum.

- Your payroll records, usually by quarter, then yearly by the name of your employee and his or her class code. Break out overtime and tips
- Your profit and loss or other financial accounting records
- Your federal tax returns
- A certificate of insurance for each subcontractor that covers the project dates
- Detailed descriptions of the role performed by each employee in the class code assigned to that employee

Most insurers now complete audits entirely by email. One insurance expert believes that errors occur in over 75 percent of today's workers' compensation audits. Trust me, these errors rarely occur in your favor.

You'll probably never meet your auditor. In fact, they're often in another state or work for a premium audit company unrelated to your insurer. Therefore, there's little chance to build a relationship with the auditor. Still, it pays to be timely and polite when you provide information.

Never Ignore Your Audit

If you refuse to respond to an audit, your insurer considers you "unresponsive." You agree to the audit when you buy the policy, even if you didn't read your insurance contract. You're breaking a promise and a policy condition if you fail to respond. Auditors don't go away.

Here's what can happen if you ignore your annual audit.

- Your insurer usually will cancel your current policy because the audit covers your previous year. This can be damaging to any business owner because your agent has to explain to a potential insurer that you failed to meet a policy condition.

- Whether or not your insurer cancels your policy, your insurer will complete an estimated audit, based on the insurer's best guess. Usually, the estimated audit can be from 25 percent to 300 percent of the original premium. That hurts.

- After your insurer estimates your audit, they will send you an additional premium invoice that covers the previous audit year.

o If you don't pay that premium, your insurer will turn your account over to a collection agency.

o Your insurer may sue you, especially if they feel you may have deliberately misclassified employees or acted fraudulently in some other manner.

o Your insurer will notify advisory organizations of your actions, such as the NCCI, which may disqualify you from obtaining workers' compensation coverage elsewhere.

I Owe How Much?

Upon the insurer's audit completion, you may owe an additional premium. If you encounter problems with your audit, call your insurance agent or broker immediately. This is one of the main reasons you want a skilled agent or broker who understands the entire workers' compensation process, not just how to report your premium to you.

Audit errors often include the following.

- Misclassifying your business's class code
- Improperly classifying employees, usually to a higher-rated class code
- Errors in excluded payroll, including overtime, depending

on your state's rules

- Opinions regarding subcontractors classified as employees
- Applying an incorrect emod or an emod from the wrong period
- Refusing to furnish you with audit worksheets, which outline your business and employee class
- Recalculating the rates charged initially by the insurer, generating additional premium

If your agent can't help and you believe the insurer miscalculated the audit, find a firm that specializes in reviewing audits and working with the insurer to correct errors. Priz helps when employers receive what he terms a "shock audit." When an audit bill for an additional premium is much higher than the original policy premium, you have a shock audit. "This seems to be a widespread problem for many smaller employers," according to Priz.

Your auditor must follow specific rules when conducting an audit. Don't undergo your audit alone. You need an experienced agent or broker who can help you through the process.

I Want To Offer You Several Important Tips.

- When you report your payroll numbers, create a spreadsheet and put annual payroll by employee next to that employee's name and class code. Very often, audits of contractors return with managers assigned to higher-rated class codes, despite breaking out the information by name, payroll and class code.
- When you receive your audit results, ensure the auditor assigned the correct employee's payroll to the correct class code. If not, you can ask why the auditor placed payroll for a manager into a higher-rated class, for example. You won't always win, especially in construction. Just because you consider a person a manager and subject to a less expensive class code doesn't mean the auditor will. If your manager drives a service truck or goes to job sites to

supervise, you're probably going to lose the argument.

- Each quarter, review your payroll and compare it to your yearly estimated premium. Issues like the recent pandemic may have significantly changed your payroll. If you're off base in your estimate at a quarter, call your agent so they can adjust your estimated payroll. Issues like overtime, bonuses, hiring more staff, or lay-offs will change your payroll. The last thing any business owner wants to face is an unexpected additional premium.

State audit rules vary, and rules that govern audits are complex. Only by keeping payroll estimates up-to-date quarterly and communicating with your broker can you avoid facing an unfavorable and costly audit.

Why Does The Auditor Want My Profit And Loss (P&L) Statements?

When reviewing the P&Ls, auditors often find errors in reported payroll because many employers continue to pay manually. They're not so concerned with your overall profit picture, so don't refuse to provide the report. Pick your battles.

Final tips on the audit

- Submit the appropriate numbers in an orderly and timely way.

- Obtain and submit certificates of insurance on independent contractors that cover the project periods.

- Review your audit upon completion. Your agent can help you interpret the audit if needed.

These tips can help you better manage this key program element.

And speaking of the pandemic, let's look at some emerging risks that will impact the future of workers' compensation.

CHAPTER FIFTEEN - EMERGING RISKS AND OPPORTUNITIES IN WORKERS' COMPENSATION

The year 2020 threw the world a curveball. Almost overnight COVID-19 changed the face of businesses, schools, governments, and industries. The workers' compensation system is vital to the smooth functioning of U.S. businesses. Yet employers and workers' compensation insurance companies face major challenges.

Challenges pose problems, but they also open opportunities to improve the workers' compensation system. Here are some of the immediate challenges and opportunities faced by today's business owners and insurers.

Covid-19 And Increasing Claims Compensability May Impact Rates

Insurers reported a decline of between 12.5 and 25 percent in workers' compensation premiums collected in 2020. This means insurers have less premium to pay claims currently on the books. Insurers are also experiencing emerging losses due to COVID-19 claims. Clearly, there is increasingly pressure on rates.

Workers' compensation laws are evolving quickly. States are passing laws that increase the number of diseases or conditions covered by workers' compensation. When passed, these laws or statutes are known as "presumptions." These include COVID-19 claims and coverage for more types of cancers sometimes affecting firefighters. COVID-19 "long haulers" are those who continue to have symptoms 28 or more days after they were first infected by COVID. Workers' compensation covered employees who are long haulers face chronic illnesses or increased disabilities. These will pose challenges for workers' compensation insurers as they seek the most informed medical providers to deliver care.

Gig Work And Work From Home Will Create Challenges And Opportunities

Our current gig and the work-from-home economy will create new challenges in claims management. The gig economy is a labor market made up mostly of those who work at home, perform freelance work, or work under short-term contracts. Many companies report that at least some of their workforce will remain at home post-pandemic. Less money spent on employee benefits and commercial real estate may mean more investment into a company's growth.

Technology Will Continue To Play A Significant Role In Claims And Underwriting

Health technology models such as telemedicine and artificial intelligence tools will continue to increase in workers' compensation claims management.

Technology has brought many improvements in claims handling. Here are two.

1.   Social media investigations of injured claimants. A number of companies have sprung up that specialize in mining social media to verify the injured employee's activity level.

2.   Data mining to indicate which employees might be more likely to malinger.

Additionally, insurers increasingly rely on predictive modeling to set rates and determine which accounts they can write profitably. Predictive analytics takes statistical and analytical information to develop models that predict future outcomes. To set their rates, today's underwriters use sophisticated predictive models built on big data. Using modeling, underwriters quickly know how much premium they need to charge to make a profit on your business. Underwriters still use your emod and it still appears on your information page. However, according to Pennachio, "The emod no longer has a direct influence on premiums. Basically, the insurer's model tells underwriters how much to charge, and then they work backward to accommodate the emod."

That is not to say your emod isn't important; it is. It helps organizations track their loss experience, and it is critical for contractors who must meet emod requirements to bid on contracts.

However, the emod formula is 100 years old, Pennachio reminds us. Today's predictive modeling, driven by big data and the large data sets now readily available to insurers, can provide underwriters with a quicker and more impersonal approach to rate decisions.

Improved Safety And Loss Prevention Practices Will Decrease Losses While Claims Costs Will Rise

Improved safety and loss prevention practices such as better personal protective equipment and programs that monitor driver behavior will continue to reduce losses.

Claim costs will increase. Medical inflation continues to outstrip general inflation, with no end in sight. Managing care from the first report of injury through claim conclusion can help insurers reduce lost time and decrease medical costs. Again, some states do not allow medical management. The employee or his or her attorney directs the care. Obtaining the best-in-class medical treatment for employees saves costs by preventing permanent total disability and reducing lost workdays.

An Evolving Population Will Create More Claims Challenges

An aging population and a population with more mental health challenges will make claims management more difficult. Aging workers incur injuries less frequently than younger employees. However, they tend to take longer to heal and incur higher medical costs, according to NU Property Casualty 360. Injuries, when a worker's condition ranges from depression to suicide attempts, may require highly skilled handling. Depression from long-term unemployment or the use of opioids can delay a worker's recovery. Insurance professionals must take particular care in these cases, as well.

Racial minorities face more challenges in managing health care, including in the workers' compensation system. A 2019 study revealed a difference in treatment standards for people of color, longer delays in wage reimbursement, and poorer health outcomes. Insurers can overcome these challenges by assigning nurse case managers who can help prevent these disparities.

The Employee Advocacy Model Will Increase Among Insurers

Effective communication with injured workers will become the standard in managing workers' compensation claims. The social determinants of health (SDoH) model, also referred to as employee advocacy, will increase among enlightened insurers. Here are some of the SDoH factors.

- An employee's financial stability
- Access to transportation and food
- Home needs, such as an uncluttered environment
- Community or familial support

These SDoH variables, among others, greatly impact one's health. While these improvements may initially increase claims payments, better claims outcomes occur when employees feel valued and respected. They get well more quickly if the insurer can help address their quality-of-life needs.

Brain Drain Is Here. It Will Affect Almost Every Organization In America

Finally, the lack of incoming talent in the insurance industry will impact hiring and promotions. Brain drain in the insurance industry is a big problem, increasing the need for better training and improved communication skills. New employees may not receive adequate training. Additionally, carriers may promote adjusters into management positions before they are ready to deal with complicated claims. When I see claim denials appealed and overturned, I wonder where the supervision was on the claim. As the old saying goes, common sense is not so common.

Finally, let's review the most important steps you can take to improve your workers' compensation program.

CONCLUSION

Recapping the Steps to a Sound Workers' Compensation Program

In just a few short hours, we have explored some of the best procedures you can implement to build a first-class workers' compensation program. While we never expect injuries, we know they can and do happen. We want to do everything in our power to prevent injuries. We especially want to ensure they do not repeat. And we want to professionally manage the fallout from injuries. This can include lowered morale, required medical care, and a delayed return to work.

Here is a summary of the steps you can take to ensure a top-notch workers' compensation program.

1. Understand the benefits payable under your workers' compensation policy.

2. Know the coverage under the key sections of your workers' compensation policy.

3. Choose an agent or broker well-versed in servicing workers' compensation coverage for your type of business.

4. Develop a strong safety culture where everyone in your organization from senior management to front-line worker works safely. Hold all employees accountable for safety.

5. Bulletproof your hiring practices with thorough background checks and in-depth testing.

6. Budget for safety and workforce wellness training. Train-

ing will pay dividends if you target your efforts.

7. Investigate every injury and near-miss that occurs in your organization.

8. Develop a loss-prevention committee to investigate accidents and near misses and remedy unsafe conditions.

9. Promptly report all injuries to your insurance carrier, even those that appear minor.

10. Develop strong relationships with your claims adjusters. This means prompt, two-way communication.

11. Utilize nurse case managers to improve medical outcomes in serious or stalled claims. When one of your claims stall, suggest the insurer add a nurse to the team.

12. Institute a Stay-at-Work/Return-to-Work program that ensures your injured workers return to work as soon as possible.

13. Understand your experience modification factor. Work with your agent to ensure the NCCI or your rating bureau correctly calculates your emod to manage your premiums.

14. Apply the tips on audit response to survive your yearly premium audit.

15. Scan the environment for emerging risks. Don't let the future blindside you.

These tips can help you manage the most important parts of your workers' compensation program. It will mean fewer injuries, lower premiums, and a more profitable future for your business.

GLOSSARY OF WORKERS' COMPENSATION TERMS

Adjuster or examiner – The person working for the insurer or a third-party administrator who manages the injured employee's claim, usually throughout the life of the injury. An independent adjuster (i/a) may complete the initial claim investigation; however, the independent adjuster works for a firm that specializes in field investigations.

AOE/COE – Acronyms for "arising out of employment' and occurring during the "course of employment. This is a two-pronged test for determining claim compensability. For AOE, the injury must arise due to a work-related activity. For COE, the employee must be in the course of his or her employment duties when the incident occurs.

Assigned risk insurance plan – When states require insurance such as workers' compensation coverage, risks that unacceptable in the standard insurance market must have an alternative to find coverage. Many call workers' compensation assigned risk plans the market of "last resort." According to one workers' compensation expert, approximately 10 percent of all insured employers are in assigned risk plans.

Average weekly/monthly wage (AWW/AMW) – The pre-earning ability of an employee based on the amount s/he earned preceding the injury. This rate determines the employee's rate of temporary total or temporary partial disability, or his or her permanent total disability, when applicable. The calculation varies by state.

Class code – The duties of the position and its risk helps to determine the employee's class code. These are three- or four-digit codes that assign a rate to a position. Most states use codes established by the National Council on Compensation Insurance (NCCI). Some states use their own class codes.

Comorbidities – Medical issues that preexist the injury or illness and that may exacerbate the employee's work injury or illness, complicating healing.

Compensability – Once the adjuster determines an injury is indeed work-related injury, they refer to it as compensable.

Date of injury (DOI) or date of accident (DOA) – The date the incident occurred. If that date cannot be determined exactly, the adjuster will estimate the DOI.

Date of report (DOR) – The date the carrier receives notice of the claim, or the date the employer received notice of the claim.

Employee (EE) – The injured employee. Often abbreviated as EE in reports.

Employer – The hiring entity. Often abbreviated as ER in reports.

Endorsement – A form attached to your policy that changes or adds wording that alters your insurance policy. Endorsements can add, eliminate, or alter coverage found in the policy. In addition to reading your policy, you should carefully review all policy endorsements attached to or listed on your coverage form.

Essential job functions – Basic job duties an employee must be able to perform either with or without reasonable accommodation. For example, lifting 25 pounds may be an essential job function. Your job descriptions should spell out all essential job functions before you advertise or hire for the job.

Experience modification factor – Rating agencies develop this factor by measuring your actual past loss experience by the expected or actual experience of your class of business. This factor can be a debit or a credit. For example, a 1.02 factor means your experience will increase your premium, while a factor below 1.0 will decrease your premium.

Functional capacity evaluation (FCE) – A series of testing administered by a highly trained physical therapist or a physician to determine the employee's ability to perform his or her job functions. That medical provider furnishes a written report, which describes physical capabilities and restrictions. The FCE should provide an objective evaluation of your employee's ability or lack of ability to perform his or her essential job functions. If the employee or the attorney representing your employee disagrees with the report, they can obtain their own report. FCEs should follow nationally standardized protocols and testing methods.

First report of injury (FROI) – After an on-the-job injury or illness, the employer completes the FROI and immediately sends it to the insurer. The insurer forwards the form to the state agency. However, many states require the employer to file the FROI with the state directly, not relying on the carrier. Determine the procedure your insurance carrier recommends. If you refuse to file a FROI on behalf of an injured employee, most states allow the injured employee to file in his or her own behalf. It's best, if you disagree with the injury details, to inform your insurer and allow your carrier to file and dispute the claim. Never simply ignore an employee's complaint of injury or illness.

Future medical costs – State law typically requires employers to pay future medical expenses arising from a job-related injury or illness. Some states allow an estimation of those expenses and a payment to close the claim. Often years later, employees will ask the state to reopen a claim for an injury that again requires treatment.

Independent medical examination (IME) – The IME is a tool to assess your employee's physical condition or whether an employee's injury occurred as a result of his or her job duties. An independent physician conducts the exam and has no treating relationship with the employee.

Indemnity claim – Any injury or illness claim where the insurer pays benefits beyond medical payments. These benefits can include lost wages, permanent partial or permanent total disability, or death benefits.

Impairment rating – The percentage of use your injured employee has lost due to an injury or illness. For example, losing a great toe creates a certain level of impairment. The insurer's physician bases these ratings on guidelines the American Medical Association publishes. The physician can assign the rating to a body part, or to the body as a whole. The rating then helps the industrial commission to determine permanent partial disability benefits owed to your employee post loss.

Injury frequency – The number of injuries per 1,000,000 employee hours worked. In simple terms, how often your injuries occur to your employees.

Injury severity – The number of workdays lost x 200,000 divided by the employee total hours worked.

Lag time – The time period between the date of the injury and when the workers' compensation insurer receives the first report of injury.

Large deductible plan – Large, usually multi-state employers may decide to institute a deductible plan for their workers' compensation coverage. Deductibles generally are between $100,000 to $1,000,000 per occurrence. The insurer handles the claims then the insured reimburses the insurer for amount paid under the deductible.

Light duty (LD) – Rarely used to avoid the appearance of creating a permanent position. See "temporary modified duty."

Life expectancy – The term used as a factor to determine what future benefits the insurer may owe in claims of total permanent disability.

Maximum medical improvement (MMI) – The ultimate goal in treating an employee's injury. The employee reaches MMI when his or her condition is as good as it's going to get, in layperson's terms. At MMI, the employee may still need medical treatment, but that treatment will not normally improve his or her condition. Once the employee reaches MMI, the insurer can normally suspend temporary total benefits and resolve any medical permanency.

Nurse case manager – Nurse case managers help to coordinate the best medical benefits for injured employees. They should be employee advocates, helping locate the best physicians and medical practitioners for the type of injury. They may attend your employees' doctor appointments and help to schedule procedures such as testing and surgery with appropriate medical providers.

Permanent partial disability (PPD) – After an injury, an employee may have some physical impairment. The state helps to calculate the PPD benefits owed in accordance with its statutes. This amount varies by the level of impairment and the body part impaired.

Permanent total disability (PTD) – After an injury, some employees cannot return to productive employment. PTD payments are often for the life of the injured employee and are usually two-thirds of the employee's average weekly or monthly wage. By providing the best medical care, adjusters do everything in their power to prevent this finding. However, in catastrophic injuries, this may not be possible.

Stay at Work/Return to work (SAW/RTW) – Proactive strategies utilized by employers to keep an employee working after an injury to decrease wage loss and prevent long-term disability. This can include modifying the employee's original position or creating SAW/RTW duties such as answering phones, studying safety procedures, or other tasks injured employees can perform within their medical restrictions.

Subrogation – The right the insurer has to pursue a third party who caused or contributed to your employee's injury or illness.

Temporary modified duty – An assignment for a specific and short period that allows an injured employee to perform some job within his or her ability to work rather than stay at home.

Third-party administrator (TPA) – Larger employers may choose to take higher deductibles or retentions on their workers' compensation coverage. They then face to task of processing their employees' injury and illness claims. Many larger self-insured organizations hire a TPA to administer any claims on their behalf.

Temporary modified duty (TMD) – Often referred to as "light duty," this is the time period in which the employer accommodates the employee so that s/he is able to perform some functions at work. A written agreement should, at a minimum, specify the time period, the name of the person to whom the employee reports and a statement outlining the consequences if the employee refuses to accept the temporary assignment. The injured employee should sign or decline the agreement in writing.

Temporary partial disability (TPD) – After an injury when an employee is unable to perform his or her normal duties, TPD smooths earning between what the employee could have made and what s/he is making.

Temporary total disability (TTD) – An injured employee who cannot work receives TTD benefits while s/he recovers. Each state outlines the amount of benefits subject to a maximum. Generally, TTD benefits equal two-thirds of the employee's average weekly or monthly wage subject to a minimum or maximum amount. Once an employee reaches MMI or can return to work, the carrier will normally stop paying TTD.

Unit Statistical Report – Also called a "stat report" or "stat card," this provides the NCCI with your organization's payroll and loss information so that they can assign your company with an experience modification factor.

Utilization review (UR) – An assessment available in many states to determine whether the types and amounts of medical treatment are medically necessary. UR is an attempt by the insurer to reduce medical costs when appropriate.

Vocational benefits – Some states require vocational benefits when an employee cannot return to his or her original occupation. Some carriers while not required by statute to offer vocational benefits will do so to assist the injured worker and to ultimately save costs.

Vocational expert – An expert in vocational rehabilitation retained by either the employee or the insured to determine an employee's capability in performing work functions. The vocational expert often prepares a written report and rates the employee's estimated loss of future earnings.

Workers' Compensation Medicare Set-Aside Arrangement (WCMSA or MSA) – A WCMSA is "a financial agreement that allocates a portion of a workers' compensation settlement to pay for future medical services related to the workers' compensation injury, illness, or disease. Simply put, Medicare does not want to pay for the medical expenses that the employer's insurer should pay. Medicare and the carrier determine the set-aside amount on a case-by-case basis. Hammering out an agreement with Medicare may delay closing the claim.

ABOUT THE AUTHOR

Nancy Germond

Nancy Germond is the President of Insurance Writer, a consulting firm located in Pheonix, Arizona. With more than three decades of risk management experience, her unique insights and abilities help businesses better understand and manage their risk. Nancy has authored scores of risk management-related articles, white papers, and has consulted and presented to both public sector and private sector insurance organizations.

A second-generation insurance professional, Nancy was the first risk manager for the City of Prescott, Arizona, and has worked in the private and public sectors as a claim and risk manager. In 1997 she founded Insurance Writer to assist insurance organizations to better manage their employment-related issues and to better penetrate the competative insurance marketplace. Nancy holds a B.A. in Communications from Mills College and a Masters degree in Sociology from Lincoln University. She also holds the Associate in Risk Management and the Associate in Claims designations from the Insurance Institute of America, the Insurance Training Professional designation from the Society of Insurance Trainers and Educators, and is a Senior Professional in Human Resource Management.

Nancy and her husband own a plumbing contracting company in Glendale, Arizona

Made in the USA
Middletown, DE
13 February 2024